Judith Dimond is a lay member of St Martin's and St Paul's Church in Canterbury, and a Companion of the Society of St Francis. She had two careers, one in equal opportunities and earlier in advice giving, and on retiring she began writing. She is part of a lively group – Common Room Poets – which has produced two anthologies, and performs locally. She is also published in several poetry journals. Her family life encompasses four generations from 97 to 4, and she's somewhere in the top half. She lives with her husband in what was once a pub, and together they enjoy exploring the coasts of Kent and northern France. She is also the author of *Gazing on the Gospels, Year B* and *Gazing on the Gospels, Year C* (SPCK 2008, 2009).

GAZING ON
THE GOSPELS
YEAR A

Meditations on the Lectionary readings

Judith Dimond

First published in Great Britain in 2010

Society for Promoting Christian Knowledge
36 Causton Street
London SW1P 4ST
www.spckpublishing.co.uk

British Library Cataloguing-in-Publication Data
A catalogue record for this book is available from the British Library

ISBN 978–0–281–06188–4

1 3 5 7 9 10 8 6 4 2

Typeset by Graphicraft Ltd, Hong Kong
Printed in Great Britain by MPG

Produced on paper from sustainable forests

Contents

Acknowledgements

With grateful thanks to Sister Frances Teresa Downing osc, without whom this book would never have been started, and Reverend Canon Paul Cox, without whom this book would never have been finished.

Introduction

In her Fourth Letter to Agnes, St Clare of Assisi described Jesus as a 'mirror without blemish'. Just imagine how marvellous such a mirror would have seemed in the twelfth century. Before the advent of glass mirrors, all reflections were plagued by distortions. As a rich young woman, before her conversion, Clare must have gazed in many a flawed mirror, just as teenage girls and boys do today, spending hours looking at themselves, questioning and rehearsing their identity. As Sister Clare, what she wanted for her followers was for them to capture in prayer that intense concentration, yet without the vanity. For the mirror she called us all to gaze into reveals to us Christ, and ourselves only as seen in him.

At some points in her writing, St Clare lets the verbs tumble over each other in her insistence – ponder, see, contemplate, look, consider: she repeats them again and again. In her Second Letter, Clare leaves us with a clearer instruction:

> *Gaze*
> *Consider*
> *Contemplate*
> *As you desire to imitate him*

And it is this structure that is followed in these reflections on the weekly Gospels of the Revised Common Lectionary.

Using Clare's template allows us the chance to be stimulated through our senses, through our feelings and our minds, and through our hearts, so engaging the whole person in the act of prayerful study. The purpose behind these reflections is to provoke readers to ask themselves: what does this story stimulate in me today? What might it mean to others outside my own small circle? I have tried to make each piece appropriately personal, yet accessible. More than anything, I want to link the sacred and the secular, or rather to demolish the false dichotomy we so often impose – perhaps we hope that way to keep the gospel safe, and reduce its power in the world.

Though Year A is the first in the lectionary, this volume is the last of the cycle to be written. But the value of any cycle is that it is circular, as is the value of the teaching of St Clare, who always returns us to Jesus, yet keeps us involved in our own relationships and responsibilities. 'God's love is never closed in upon itself' (Claire Marie Ledoux, *Clare of Assisi: Her Spirituality Revealed in Her Letters*, trans. Colette Joly Dees, Cincinnati, OH: St Anthony Messenger Press, 2003).

> The image of the mirror speaks of a kind of infectious spirituality, in which what is seen in prayer, in gazing, in contemplation, effects a transformation in the life of the one who gazes, so that others may be drawn by what they see in her to their own contemplation, and to their own transformation.
>
> (Helen Julian CSF, *Living the Gospel*,
> Abingdon: Bible Reading Fellowship, 2001)

If we have truly gazed, considered and contemplated the good news, we will surely be compelled to change, and so the final prayer of each piece will often challenge us to action in imitation of Jesus. It is no coincidence that the four Gospels of the New Testament are followed immediately by *The Acts* of the Apostles. The true value of these reflections must be measured by the degree to which they have provoked, nudged or encouraged us to imitate our Lord.

ADVENT

The First Sunday of Advent

Matthew 24.36–44

Gaze on Noah – who is this man? Though he's a righteous person, he's by no means perfect, as we discover after the flood subsides – for the last time we see him, he is drunk and naked! But we are told he 'walked with God'. Like Mary, mother of Jesus millennia later, he is God's chosen instrument. And like Mary, Noah is obedient. He listens to God's absurdly detailed instructions for the building of the Ark and doesn't protest that he knows very well how to put together a watertight boat, and why is God being so particular? He listens to God's judgement on the peoples of the world without a murmur of defence. He doesn't argue with God's harshness or ask 'why me?' We are told that 'Noah did everything just as God commanded him'.

And what is more, he did it speedily. Noah becomes our first example of staying awake, trustful and obedient to God.

Consider how, after the Nativity, the story of Noah is probably the most popular to tell to children. Look at all the pretty picture books and jigsaws, models and felt toys of the animals which we give to our children to play with. But the procession of delightful animals two by two, and the pretty rainbow are the 'happy ending'. The story begins when we hear God's discovery that humankind's 'heart was only evil . . . [for] . . . all people of the earth had corrupted their ways . . . and the earth is filled with violence' (Genesis 6.5, 12, 13). As it still is today.

Consider how this gospel reading for the first Sunday of the year is a warning which shows us Jesus in as stern a mood as God in Genesis. We are not allowed to ease ourselves gently into the new liturgical year, nor are we allowed to drift cheerfully to Christmas. We are warned of catastrophe and destruction and an almost random judgement. There is no reference to God's love or compassionate nature. We cannot avoid this element of threat within the Gospel, and must wrestle with its meaning.

But we know that those who listened to Jesus telling the beginning of Noah's story also knew the end. Consider God's words to Noah when the flood had subsided and he came out of the Ark: 'Never again will I curse the ground because of man, *even though* every inclination of his heart is evil from childhood' (Genesis 8.21). In other words, God does not pretend that this 'second' creation is any better than the first. We are not improved by the flood, but God is resolved to love us in our weakness and corruption. And so he establishes his first covenant with humankind, and the rainbow as its sign.

Consider how at the beginning of Advent we look forward to the New Covenant, where a star will be the sign in the heavens, just as the rainbow was the sign of the First Covenant.

We do not know if we would have been in Noah's family, safe in the ark, or left to drown in the deluge. Nor do we know which of the two men or women in the field we will be. But we can stay awake, obedient and trusting, as Noah did.

Contemplate a waiting that is mixed with dread, just as Noah waited for the flood. Contemplate a waiting filled with excitement and hope, just as Noah waited for the dove to return. Contemplate how similar yet how different the feelings of dread and excitement are. Note how both have equal prominence in the stories ahead of us this year. A dread which is born of a world out of joint with God's will, and an excitement born out of God's promises that he will rescue us.

As you desire to imitate him

My God and my Judge, may I walk through the days of Advent
Obedient and trusting as Noah,
With a listening which is also an act of obedience,
A wakefulness that is also a prayer,
Always living my life in hopeful expectation
Of the Second Coming.
Amen.

The Second Sunday of Advent

Matthew 3.1–12

Gaze on harvest time in ancient Canaan: the whole community must work hard together to bring in the grain. First the men cut down the ripened grain, gripping their hand sickles till they get blisters. Then the women must bind the barley or wheat into sheaves, much like those we used to see in our fields, before those ugly black plastic wraps became commonplace. Watch them bending and straightening, bending and straightening, mopping their brows in the warm air.

Then the grain is carted back to the open air threshing floor, where it is loosened from the straw, sometimes by the heavy tread of cattle. The site has been specially chosen because it is exposed to the prevailing winds. By now, it is late afternoon, and the breeze has risen in time for the grain to be winnowed. Up in the air they toss the grain, straining their shoulders, so that the wind will blow away the straw and chaff, leaving the heavier grain at the winnower's feet. This is the grain that they can use; this is the grain that is good.

The wind is vital to this operation, for without it, the good grain could not be collected. John the Baptist is telling us this is just like the Holy Spirit, not always gentle and mild, but sifting, and judging. For the last job of the harvest was to burn the chaff.

Consider how glibly we use the metaphor of the wheat and the chaff when we want to judge others, and divide them into the 'approved' and the 'disapproved'. In today's Old Testament lesson, from Isaiah, we heard how, when God's plans reach fulfilment, the lion and the ox, the bear and the cow, the wolf and the lamb, and the leopard and the kid, will all lie down together. So we learn that God's plan is for the kingdom of heaven to be inclusive. God does not choose to exclude us, but so often, we exclude ourselves by thinking we are better than others, or purer, or more righteous. Just like the Pharisees and the Sadducees, in fact. Consider how God is teaching that we must be prepared to share the kingdom with unlikely bedfellows.

Consider how John, in common with all prophets, meant his message to be for us as a community, as well as individuals. It is often the collective choices made by a society which show our real values. We cannot blame the economic crisis of 2009 on a few bankers; we must be honest about our complicity and repent. We cannot hide behind our church membership and say we didn't subscribe to greed. What did we actually do to change people's hearts and minds? 'Do not think you can say to yourselves, "We have Abraham as our father"' (Matthew 3.9), said John.

Contemplate how short Advent is. We have only four weeks to prepare for the kingdom. But if we had longer, would we be any more prepared? Sense the urgency in this reading. We are told to repent now.

Contemplate how you are preparing for Christmas: when you write your cards, do you dash them off in a hurry without a thought for the person you are sending them to? Or do you think of each person in turn, and contemplate what they mean in your life, and how they have played a part in your life's journey, and give thanks?

As you desire to imitate him

Dear Lord, help me to prepare for your coming
By making space and staying still.
Help me to prepare by honest examination of myself.
Help me to lift my face to the wind of your Spirit
And be prepared for your judgement.
Amen.

The Third Sunday of Advent

Matthew 11.2–11

Gaze on John's disciples. We don't know their names, but we can imagine a group a little like the disciples that Jesus chose, all shapes and sizes, and drawn from all walks of life. They are a faithful band who have shared with him the rigours of the desert and the sternness of his message, and not been put off. They have hoped great things of him, and even thought he might be Elijah, or even 'the one to come' himself. But John has always insisted otherwise, and pointed away from himself, towards another.

And now John is in prison, and it looks as if his purposes are doomed, along with John himself. John seems to weaken, and doubts himself, for now he sends his disciples off to Jesus. Before he dies, as he fears he will, he's desperate to know if the struggle has all been worthwhile. Watch the disciples meet with Jesus. What is going on in their heads? They must be thinking, what's so special about this man? Can he be the one John has predicted? Will he be any more reliable than John?

Consider how Jesus doesn't start with promises or predictions, but with evidence based on how he is fulfilling the words of another prophet, namely Isaiah. And then he goes on to reaffirm John in the mind of his disciples, for he tells them to carry on with their support of him, and he insists he was indeed a truly great prophet – not a reed bending in the wind, but someone upright and unyielding. So he confirms their loyalty to John and eases their confusion, and their fear that his life may have been in vain.

Consider how important it is in all our lives to know that what we set out to do was worthwhile, and that we have not chased after a dream. Or rather, that the dream was a worthy one. Consider the difference between a dream which is merely a wish, and a dream that is a vision. Our wishes may be trivial hopes, not relevant to ourselves or appropriate to our lives. How I wish I could ski, or sing a church solo – they chop and change from day to day. Our visions must be stronger than these, based on our ideals and our values, and rooted in God's word, able to sustain us through challenges.

Contemplate what is the dream that dominates your life. Is your dream rooted in the kingdom of heaven? If so, no fame or fortune will be necessary to make your heart glad, for you can count upon being as great as John the Baptist himself; or as insignificant.

And if your dream is rooted in Christ, no imprisonment or persecution will be a stumbling block. And you will be prepared to wait with faith for the dawning of the kingdom.

As you desire to imitate him

Dear Lord, may I have the strength of John the Baptist
To withstand persecution.
May I share John's vision
And see the signs and preach the way.
Then grant me his humility,
So that I accept the part you would have me play,
However small, in the coming of the kingdom.
Amen.

The Fourth Sunday of Advent

Matthew 1.18–25

Gaze on Joseph, the day his world turns upside down. It's just like a TV soap – the cheated husband, the penitent wife, and the shocked neighbours. Though inside Joseph must have been furious, he doesn't seem the type to rant and rave. Angry and hurt, his first thought must have been that she had been unfaithful.

Gaze on him pacing up and down the hillside around Nazareth, refusing to come in for supper. He churns over his distress, wishing the clock could be turned back to a time before he'd ever proposed to Mary or even met her. Hear him rehearsing how he is going to tell his family that the wedding is off. Gaze on the fading light as dusk approaches, and feel the first shiver of the night. See him go inside, his shoulders slumped, his head bowed. First he tries to calm his mind, by picking up his chisel and getting on with his jobs by the dim, flickering oil lamp. But that doesn't help and eventually a huge weariness comes over him. He lies on his bed, pulls the blanket over himself, and sighs.

Perhaps it will be clearer in the morning.

Consider Joseph's predicament. He certainly deserves our sympathy. He is a righteous Jew, concerned to uphold the laws and customs of his world. And those laws say he should divorce Mary, although he's only betrothed to her, and leave her to carry the shame of an illegitimate child. But God intervenes, and this very ordinary person does an extraordinary thing – he takes Mary to his home, completes the marriage contract and acknowledges the child as his.

Consider the example of forgiveness that Joseph demonstrated to all around; consider the risk he took of being shamed himself.

And if the 'true' story was ever revealed, he would become a laughing stock, as well as a cuckold.

Consider how, here, at the very beginning of Jesus' life, we see two of the principles of Jesus' later teaching – the first, to be slow to judge, and generous in forgiveness. And the second: do not cling to rules for the sake of appearances or through fear of the priestly hierarchy, but practise mercy.

Is it at all possible that Joseph told Jesus this story when he grew up, and that as Jesus pondered it, he drew these lessons from his own remarkable beginning?

Contemplate the various ways in which God reveals himself in this short passage – through a dream (might we call this spiritual alertness?), and through an angel (might we see this as the intervention of a trusted messenger?) and through the Old Testament prophets (we might call this the word of God).

Contemplate how God most readily reveals himself to you. Is it through your own innermost dreams and prayers, or through the mediation of others, or through Scripture?

As you desire to imitate him

Dear Father, may I imitate the trust Joseph put in you
And the mercy and love he showed to Mary.
Enable me to do extraordinary things for you
So that I may provide a safe place
For your birth this Christmas.
Amen.

CHRISTMAS

Christmas Day

Luke 2.1–14

Gaze on all the people in Bethlehem that day who were unaware of what was going on under their noses. They didn't give the stable a second glance. See the baker up all night, making the bread for the rich families, and sweet honey cakes, ready for a little girl's fifth birthday. Gaze on the little girl, waking with excitement on her special day. Hear the sounds coming from the carpenter's workshop, as the workman puts the finishing touches to a coffin, ready for the funeral of an old man later that day. Hear the sobbing and crying of that family.

Smell the dirt of the donkeys, penned in overnight, having too brief a rest before they begin their working day. Hear the rich merchant bustling about, calling to his servants to get everything ready for his journey to the coast. Watch as the shepherds' wives light their fires, and wonder what kind of a night their husbands have had, up on the chill and bleak mountainside.

Yet another day for ordinary people, all suffering with the over-crowding caused by the census, vexed by the worries that each day brings, struggling on with the same hopes that life will turn out all right in the end.

Consider who were the first to greet the baby – maybe the innkeeper's wife was curious, and popped her head round the door when she heard the cry, but she wasn't anyone of any great note. And then there were the shepherds, who didn't own land or have any stake in the running of their town, or any standing in the synagogue.

Consider who were not invited – the local landowner was over-looked, as was the captain of the nearest Roman fort. No priests were summoned from Jerusalem, not even the lay elders from the local synagogue appeared. This was not a 'black tie' event. Consider who today may have been invited to the manger – those without a stake in the outcome, who could not control it.

Consider how things might have turned out if after all, from the first day of Jesus' life, he'd been recognized and honoured and cared for (a little like the Dalai Lamas were in Tibet). Wouldn't God's plan have been easier? Wouldn't everyone have believed from the start? Consider why God wanted his son to grow up in obscurity and remain hidden until he decided it was time to reveal him.

One of the reasons was, surely, to protect him from Herod and all the other vested interests who would want to prevent him carrying out his destiny, or else would have fought over him and tried to manipulate him for their own ends. But a more positive reason may have been that God needed Jesus to identify totally with ordinary, flawed humanity, and not be cocooned or removed from ordinary life. Jesus had to experience the reality of the world his Father had created.

Contemplate God's desire that this baby breathe with his breath, yet think with the mind of a man and love with the heart of a mother.

Contemplate the miracle of the incarnation: God wrote his DNA into the baby, born in a stable. Contemplate how God gave Jesus his own fingerprints, so that whatever Jesus touched, we know God has touched too.

As you desire to imitate him

Dear Jesus, may I be invited to the manger
And welcomed in the stable;
With the angels may I sing your praises,
With the shepherds may I kneel and adore,
And as you grew into the likeness of your Father
May I grow into a likeness of you.
Amen.

The First Sunday of Christmas

Matthew 2.13–23

Gaze on old black and white newsreel of Jewish refugees in the 1930s, stumbling bleary-eyed from trains in the UK or landing bewildered from trans-Atlantic ships in New York. In one hand they clutch a battered suitcase, and in the other, they clasp the small hand of their child. They look around with startled expressions at this foreign country which is reluctantly giving them safety. How difficult to really understand the devastation they must have felt at losing everything. The signs at the docks were in a different language, and the staff wore a strange costume. Listen as hard as they could, they only heard a babble of nonsense. They were offered tea with milk, and eggs with bacon, without any regard for their kosher laws. The father had no way to earn tomorrow's meal; the mother nowhere to make a bed for the children.

Nothing was certain in their lives any more, except that there was no going back.

Consider the way Matthew uses the Old Testament in this gospel passage. Again and again he refers back to it to prove his case. From Hosea he plucks the line 'Out of Egypt I have called my Son'. By choosing this, Matthew draws parallels between the nation of Israel, once exiled in Egypt and freed at the Exodus, and this one individual Jew in whom the history of Israel is encapsulated, and is to be vindicated.

Next, he considers Rachel, the wife of Jacob and the mother of two of the tribes of Israel, weeping as her descendants are driven into exile. Here he is empathizing with the mothers of Bethlehem, grieving over the massacre of the innocents.

Finally, Matthew ends with the enigmatic quote 'He will be called a Nazarene' – which Bible scholars have not been able to find in the Old Testament! It is as if Matthew's determination to link Jesus with the history of his people has carried him away. In this, the most 'Jewish' of all the Gospels, Matthew strives to show how the biography of Jesus 'fulfilled what the Lord had said through the prophet'. He is determined that we interpret Jesus' life correctly, as completing God's plan. And God's plan is that Jesus must grow up to carry out his adult ministry, and so he is protected from the fury of Herod. But this very early childhood experience will have marked Jesus for ever, and for ever made him able to empathize with the outsider, the refugee, and the outcast, and with the history of his people. For from the migration of Abraham, through the Exodus from Egypt to the Babylonian captivity, their story was one of movement and exile.

Contemplate your own sense of security. Even if we have not been refugees ourselves, we may know them in our neighbourhoods – Iraqis and Afghans today, Ugandans a generation ago. All of us at one time will experience the insecurity of ill-health and grief. Contemplate how at these times, your world turns upside down, and there is no handrail to keep you steady. Even though you keep a roof over your head, and food in the fridge, you feel lost, adrift and powerless.

Contemplate where your real security lies – place it in the love of God, which will never let you down or cast you out, but will go into exile with you.

As you desire to imitate him

Dear Father, may I trust in you to uphold me
   When my world is falling apart,
And trust in you to defend me
   When I feel threatened by others,
And trust in you to protect me
   When I am all alone;
Through the love of God which will follow me
   Wherever I flee.
Amen.

The Second Sunday of Christmas

John 1.[1–9] 10–18

Gaze – a little late in the calendar, but it should still be fresh in your memory – on the children's stocking, that dangled at the foot of the bed, or was hung up at the fireplace, on Christmas Eve, and now bulges with goodies. Peer at the bright red boot-shaped bag, or the knobbly old-fashioned sock, or the giant white pillowcase some families indulge in. Recall the squeals of delight; remember your own great excitement as a child, delving into the stocking on Christmas morning. You plunged your hand into the mysterious depths and wriggled it right round the heel up to the toe, anxious to explore and discover every single present, to the very last gold chocolate coin. It never occurred to you that you didn't deserve all this generosity. Nor did it cross your mind that the gift would not be good.

Consider how we become 'children of God' (v. 12). Are we born into God's family or are we adopted at baptism? Or do we actually have to adopt God as our Father in order to become his child? All three exchanges seem to be occurring in this passage. Think about what gives us 'the right' to become his child. Here we are told it is when we recognize and receive him, in and through the One and Only Jesus, the Word made flesh.

In a sense we adopt God when we recognize and receive him, for only then do we name him Father. Children who are adopted share no biological or genetic inheritance with their legal parent but in those families where the adoption goes well, and love is reciprocated, the adopted child may grow to walk or talk like the parent and share their values and outlook. At some point he or she will understand what it means for them to have been adopted and at that point they

16

make a mature decision that 'you are my real parent'. What joy that must be for the parent who took such a risk!

The idea of adoption is made explicit in today's epistle: 'in love he predestined us to be adopted as his sons [and daughters]' (Ephesians 1.4–5). That word 'predestined' may make many of us feel uncomfortable, but considering Paul's past life of opposition to the new way adhered to by the followers of Jesus, and the persecution he had pursued, it is quite understandable that he of all people might believe his conversion was predestined, and totally out of his control.

Contemplate the world around you and look for the signs that help you recognize 'the word made flesh'. It may be in the beauty of creation – at this time of year, frost on the ground, or snow on the trees, but it should be more than that. Look for the signs in the people around you: the grace of forgiveness, the power of truthfulness, the love of lives dedicated to others. Contemplate times in your life when you have known the presence of the One and Only.

As you desire to imitate him

Creator God, may I recognize your word made flesh
And receive through your grace the blessings
You have planned for me since the beginning of time.
Through my belief in your name
May I become your child and call you Father,
Through your One and Only Son, Jesus Christ.
Amen.

EPIPHANY

The First Sunday of Epiphany

Matthew 3.13–17

Gaze on Jesus standing quite unobtrusively at the edge of the crowd. He's not particularly tall, and no better dressed than anyone else. There's nothing in his appearance that would single him out at all. He's on his own, for so far he's collected no disciples. He's just left Nazareth for a visit to his cousin John; and his parents worry that maybe the worst that might happen is that he'll join with John, who is making quite a name for himself down at the River Jordan, and stirring up the people and the authorities.

But watch him carefully – he's not joining in John's ranting and raving. For the moment he's content to be quiet and bide his time.

After a while, he begins to move forward, calmly and quietly. People look at him quizzically, but let him pass. 'Excuse me, excuse me, may I come through?', till he reaches the front. John seems to be expecting him.

Consider the long gap during which we've heard nothing of Jesus, since the family's return from Egypt. We don't know what impelled or provoked Jesus to go to the Jordan then, or whether he'd been impatient for years, or had only recently heard of John's activities and felt a stirring of intention. He appears, as he always does in his ministry, showing qualities of obedience and humility: 'it is proper' he says, when John resists the call to baptize him.

As well as obedience, here in his first adult appearance, he shows humility and subservience: to John and to God. He is putting on no airs and graces, nor making any extravagant claims. 'My Son whom I love, with whom I am well pleased' – Jesus had done nothing yet to deserve this or make sense of this claim to those around, so how does John know this to be true?

He is not beginning to speak his radical message, or teach his surprising parables. He leaves John to speak with passion about repentance – proclaiming that 'the Kingdom of Heaven is near'. In fact, it is right in front of their very eyes.

Consider how here, at the very beginning of his ministry, we are in the presence of the Trinity, which gathers in this one particular place to hallow it, and pour support on Jesus. God the Father reveals him, and God the Spirit empowers him to begin.

Contemplate the heaven opening, and the people rocking back on their heels in amazement. Contemplate how ready you are to see the signs of God's power in your world.

Contemplate the dove, how it soars with a slow beat of wings, and flies off towards the desert. And Jesus follows it, led away by the Spirit into the wilderness, to be tempted by the devil.

As you desire to imitate him

Holy Trinity, I bow before your glory.
Inspire and empower me,
Make me humble and obedient,
Help me discover what you want of me.
Wash me in the waters of baptism
And strengthen my promises
To grow in the Christian faith.
Amen.

The Second Sunday of Epiphany

John 1.29–42

Gaze on Jesus walking quietly by. We don't know where he's been, or where he's going to. It's almost as if he's 'minding his own business'. But John, who so recently baptized him, spots him immediately. Did Jesus hear him call 'Here is the Lamb of God!'? Does he smile at such recognition, or frown, thinking it is too soon for such amazing avowals?

The two disciples of John follow behind Jesus and now he turns and stops. What if he hadn't turned? Was he tempted to cling to the shadows, to remain anonymous and avoid his fate? But he doesn't hesitate, he turns immediately, for now is the time to begin.

Consider how this passage develops out of last week's, for both give accounts of the baptism of Jesus and the significance of John is underlined. But this episode concentrates on strangers being recognized and named. The recognitions are not on the superficial level, just as we might say, 'Oh, I remember him, I saw him at the bus stop yesterday.' This is God's sight acting through people, and it shows God's ability to penetrate our hearts and minds. First John recognizes Jesus as Son of God; then Andrew names him Messiah and Rabbi: the telling forth of Epiphany continues. And next, Jesus meets Simon for the first time and takes one of the great risks of his ministry: 'You will be called Cephas, Peter [Rock].'

It is worth speculating whether in fact Jesus already knew these men a little. The Gospels do not show us every minute of every day of Jesus' life – they are more like the edited highlights we get on TV of sports matches or special national events. But even if Jesus already knew them, it doesn't weaken the importance of their choice.

If we struggle to follow this rapid and enigmatic series of meetings and conversations, consider what is going on beneath the surface. What is it that prompts Jesus to ask, 'What is it you are looking for?' It is rather a direct, almost rude opening remark, and could have been said in many different tones of voice. Does Jesus instinctively respond to their restlessness and need, their lostness? Jesus doesn't just tell them where he is staying, he answers 'Come and see.' Come with me, and you will find what you are looking for.

So one by one they turn, till all the players in this story are facing the same way, towards Jesus.

Contemplate what it is *you* are looking for. Contemplate the times in your life when you have felt restless and empty, yet also excited that something new is round the corner.

Maybe this January you made some New Year Resolutions – have you been keeping them? Lent is approaching, so begin to contemplate now what disciplines you will follow, what new direction you must turn in.

Contemplate when you last heard Jesus call to you, 'Come and see.'

As you desire to imitate him

Lord, help me trust in the right people,
Look through your eyes,
And choose my friends wisely.
When you call, may I turn;
What I seek, may I find,
Through the grace of our Father.
Amen.

Dan – recognising celebs
John recognise Jesus
But more – God's sight
(Dan – artist – recognise potential ⇐⇒
What are you looking for
What (new thing) does God recognise in you

The Third Sunday of Epiphany

Matthew 4.12–23

Gaze on Jesus returning from the wilderness, where Matthew has left him in the preceding verse. His face is drawn and haggard, he's lost several pounds in weight, and his beard's untrimmed. He must have been quite a frightening sight coming over the hills to the south of Nazareth and returning home, back to the safety of family. The children would have stared at him in the street – is this Joseph's son, they ask? Where on earth has he been?

Jesus must have longed for rest and respite from the taunts and temptations he'd faced from the devil. A good bath and lots of home cooking was what he needed. But he wasn't allowed to relax for long. A passing merchant, perhaps, brings the news that John has been imprisoned and it is as if Jesus is bring driven on again. He must take up where John left off, and so, spruced up and with a picnic packed by Mary, he says goodbye and descends the hills towards Capernaum.

Consider Matthew's use of that phrase again – Jesus goes 'to fulfil what was said through the prophet'. And here he begins at last his ministry of preaching, using the same words as John: 'Repent, for the kingdom of heaven is near'. Jesus was not such a shock to the people who heard him; by and large they'd heard it all before, all the polemic about the danger the nation was in, the urgency with which they should repent, the judgement on their way of life. Today we find it much harder to make a connection between the way we live our personal lives, and the health of our nation. Earlier societies were more aware of the responsibility of the group, and less focused on the rights of the individual.

Now Matthew gives us another version of the calling of the disciples. Alone in the desert, isolated with his family in Nazareth, Jesus needs disciples to preach his message. As he meets Peter he begins to expand his preaching and paint the pictures that will so vividly explain his purposes – 'I will make you fishers of men'. In this way, this Epiphany story nudges us to place ourselves in this scene and ask ourselves to consider seriously if we'd have the courage to act as Peter, James and John did. And the sting in the tale is that they left their lives 'immediately'.

Contemplate Jesus' promise to us that the kingdom is near: it's just round the corner, tantalizingly close, if only we would take the plunge and follow him. Wherever God's rule is welcome, active and fruitful, there is the kingdom, already bubbling up like a hot spring, irrepressible, and ready to be harnessed for good. Contemplate the two possible meanings of the phrase 'for good'. One means, for benefit, and the other means, for ever. Both are true of the kingdom of heaven.

As you desire to imitate him

Dear Lord, I live in a world of shadows and threats
But you bring the promise of light.
Help me repent and turn from darkness
Towards the kingdom. Give me courage
To answer your call and become your disciple.
Amen.

The Fourth Sunday of Epiphany

John 2.1–11

Gaze on the wintry scene around you. The hills are bare and cold, the trees stark against the pale light. But although it is the end of January, snowdrops are peering out under the trees, and the startling yellow of winter jasmine is climbing round the door. Prunus blossom bursts out before its leaf, and viburnum's pink and white brightens up its dark branches. Japonica buds, like pursed kisses, are strung along the hedge already. New growth is all around us even when we least expect it. There may yet be snow and storms, but we see that spring is approaching. The secret of creation is bursting to be told, and miracles might just happen.

Consider how our world exists to be transformed. Living creatures transform from cygnet to swan, from egg to crocodile, from baby to adult. A dry bulb can produce a golden trumpet, and a dull cocoon a glorious butterfly. All is waiting to be discovered. Nothing remains static, except for stones and mountains, and even these alter imperceptibly. And here, at the end of Epiphany, when we are still struggling to church in coats and scarves, we see signs of transformation if we are only prepared to look.

Consider how Jesus came to us to transform the mess we had made of the world, so different from the good purposes of creation. Consider how, all through Epiphany, we've read stories in which other people have recognized Jesus for who he truly was. First there were kings, then a prophet – John the Baptist – and then the ordinary chaps, the disciples. But now, on the last Sunday of this season, it is Jesus' turn to show himself, and to give us a foretaste of the glory he will perform. His power can be repressed no longer.

26

Consider how he takes the water reserved for the Jews' ritual ablutions, and turns it into wine for rejoicing. He is telling us, through symbols, how the burden of the law and sin can be transformed by his free gift of life.

Consider why this, 'the first of his miraculous signs', is one of the few gospel passages that is repeated in all three years of our Lectionary. Its significance as a sign is considered as important as that. It may be just because it was his first sign, or because it refers to water and wine which means so much to us at Communion; or maybe because by this transformation, Jesus is holding out hope to us all.

Contemplate the opportunities in your life to continue the imperative of Epiphany and show Jesus to the world. Where can you proclaim him tomorrow, and how can you do that? It need not be with words, as this story so vividly shows.

Contemplate where you can start transforming situations, bringing hope and joy out of the ordinariness of daily life.

As you desire to imitate him

Transforming God, yours is the glory to be revealed
Through the power which you bestowed on Jesus.
Show me how to become a sign in the world
So that all may learn to put their trust in you
And come to know the good things you have in store.
Amen.

ORDINARY TIME

Proper 1

———◦•◦———

Matthew 5.13–20

Gaze on a city on a hill. It rises from the plain and is visible for miles. Picture, for example, the town of Rye in the very south of England, looming above Romney Marsh, almost an island left high and dry after the sea retreated. Proud and bold, the square church tower is visible to all. The road winds past irrigation canals and flocks of grazing sheep until suddenly the hill is no more, for you are at the very foot of it. From its heights you view the lives of miniature people moving about beneath you.

Or gaze on the volcanic rock of Edinburgh, with its massive castle crowning the steep slopes. Particularly gaze on it at night when all its civic buildings and houses are lit up. But if you gaze on the back streets and cellars, you'll find misdeeds and dark doings aplenty. It is difficult to tell from looking at a city on a hill, whether the souls of the residents shine.

Consider why Jesus launches into this meditation on the power of salt and light, straight after the glorious poetry of the Beatitudes. Jesus is highlighting the profound contrast between his version of the law, and the tasteless, wasted, stale version relied on by the Pharisees. That law had indeed lost its saltiness. Its flavour had vanished and its efficacy too. For salt was more important as a preservative in the ancient Mediterranean than as a mere condiment. And as a torch to show people the way, the law had become dull, and shed no light.

Consider how Matthew, from the very beginning of his Gospel, was underlining Jesus' inheritance of the Old Testament Law and Prophets. His very first verses in Chapter 1 are dedicated to the long list, which we find so boring, of the 'genealogy of Jesus Christ, Son of David, the Son of Abraham'. We skip over them, and never put them in a Sunday reading! But in Jesus' day, this genealogy was making a vital point. When we link them with Jesus' words here, 'Do not think I have come to abolish the law or the prophets', we see what Matthew is desperate to prove – that Jesus the Jew would never wish to overturn his inheritance, but to fulfil it.

For the next four weeks our reading will explore the Sermon on the Mount. Matthew's version dominates the first part of his Gospel, and even for non-Christians, it has become a beacon of wisdom. Many Christians believe that in this teaching, they hear the authentic voice of Jesus. The Blessings themselves we won't hear this year; we have to wait for Luke's version in Year C for that.

Contemplate in what ways your salt may have lost its strength; in what ways your light may have dimmed. Has the eagerness you felt when you were first a Christian faded, like a light that has been hidden? A flame when starved of oxygen will go out – where is the oxygen of your faith to be found?

As you desire to imitate him

Jesus, fulfiller of the law,
Rekindle my obedience
That I may be brought into the right way
And dwell in your kingdom with renewed righteousness.
Then will my good deeds shine to the praise of our Father.
Amen.

Proper 2

Matthew 5.21–37

Gaze on a court room in a civil case. Maybe the dispute is between neighbours about a boundary, or a business suing for an unpaid debt, or even an argument between divorced parents for custody of a child.

Listen to the arguments. Both sides believe passionately in their case, and both argue their cause, determined that their version will succeed, believing that only their story has value. Gaze on the judge, stern and inscrutable. The impartial observer will see what the parties can't: that there is right on both sides and folly on both sides.

How many times have you said about a dispute, Why don't they just sit round a table and work it out? Why can't they just speak to each other? Surely they can come to a compromise?' For the alternative to compromise is judgement. And once we put ourselves in the hands of the judge, we have no control over the outcome. We risk losing everything we fought for, and more.

Consider how this week Jesus names some of the laws that last week he commanded us to obey: do not murder, do not commit adultery. Aha! we say, that doesn't apply to us; we'd never commit such grave offences.

But Jesus is there ahead of us. His standards are much higher. Murder, he says, comes in many guises. Through anger, we murder peace, and we murder the chance of forgiveness. By deriding someone (and how many times do we sneer about someone behind their backs?), we murder their reputation, and their identity as a child of God. By committing the violence of anger and derision, we also murder our own selves, for by putting ourselves above others and our needs first, we distance ourselves from God.

Consider the high standards that Jesus insists upon. Do we really make sure we are reconciled with everyone before we 'offer our gift' – that is, ourselves – in church on Sunday? Do we really control our eyes and our hands, that covet, desire, snatch and acquire in all sorts of ways which we see as trivial, but which Jesus counts as severely as the public transgressions of murder and adultery? Our Western society has murdered the chance for millions in poorer countries which we've exploited by our greed. By lusting with our eyes, through pornography and titillation, we have murdered the decency, self-respect and integrity of women who are trafficked or prostituted for others' pleasure.

Consider again, then, the relevance of these verses to your life and your world, and your complicity in the daily murder of the dignity of the children of God.

Contemplate the people in your life who annoy you – possibly your boss, who's 'useless'; your neighbour who's 'an interfering busybody'; your colleague who's 'so lazy'. You can finish the list yourself.

Contemplate what courage it might take next time you are with friends not to descend to the usual tirade of sneer and jibe and judgement.

Contemplate the last time you lost your temper with someone. Have you been reconciled with that person yet?

As you desire to imitate him

Dear Jesus, with your help may I never participate again
In the murder of hope, or the crushing of another's dignity,
Or the extinction of love.
When my eyes lead me to desire what is not mine,
Make me blind;
When I say a cruel word, stop up my mouth;
But give me always the courage to say I'm sorry.
Amen.

Proper 3

————◦•◦————

Matthew 5.38–48

Gaze on the mugshots of criminals, or people wanted by the police or security services. Gaze on their photographs displayed on *Crime-watch* – have you seen this murderer, this rapist, this conman? His collar is crumpled, hair dishevelled, his face covered with four days of stubble, and he has a weird look in his eyes. Is it fear or defiance or just plain evil?

Picture yourself walking along by this criminal's side. Imagine him as a member of your family, or your best friend from school.

Consider the contrasts of today's Old and New Testament readings. Leviticus gives us the law – you *shall not* – fourteen times! But Jesus turns it round to a series of short positive commands: *turn, give, go, love.* Such simple words, such simple actions, but so difficult to do when they involve people who frighten or threaten us.

It is in Leviticus that we read God's injunction: 'You shall love your neighbour as yourself.' But in that passage, 'neighbour' is seen very much as your kith and kin. It is left to Jesus to enlarge the meaning and urge us to love our enemies. Jesus assumes it is obvious to everyone that this is God's nature and God's way, and he only has to quote a simple proverb in proof: 'for he makes his sun rise on the evil and the good'. Therefore, we are called to imitate the nature of God, and in these ways fulfil the law.

Consider how our world reacts when people do love their enemies. Consider the parents who forgive the murderer of their child – the press report this with a mixture of awe and incomprehension; they are happier to report those who have yet to learn God's way, and call for vengeance instead. Consider the groups of Arabs and Jews in Israel and Palestine who work together in playgroups or farming projects – there are many, but these are rarely reported. Our world is still more comfortable with Leviticus than with Jesus, and our epistle today has something to say about that: 'for the wisdom of this world is foolishness in God's sight' (1 Corinthians 3.19).

Contemplate these words by Dorothy Day, a great Roman Catholic Christian of the twentieth century. 'I really only love God as much as I love the person I love the least' (quoted by Philip Yancey in *What's So Amazing about Grace?*, Grand Rapids, MI: Zondervan, 1997).

Sit in silence for a while, and bring before God the name, the face, the actions of the person you love the least.

As you desire to imitate him

Perfect Father,
    You tell me I must love my enemy.
When next I am hurt,
    Stop me from retaliating.
When next I am cheated,
    Help me accept my loss.
May I relinquish revenge
    And embrace those I do not love,
And so grow into that perfection
    Revealed in your Son.
Amen.

The Second Sunday before Lent

Matthew 6.25–34

Gaze on the TV news one day early in January. It's the first day of the sales. The early morning queue is fidgeting, the clock moves nearer to 9 a.m., an assistant approaches and at last opens the door. The crowd, some of whom slept out on the cold winter pavement, surge in, a tsunami of greed, determined to snatch up designer dresses for a fraction of their cost, the latest plasma screen for a tenth of its price.

If you keep watching the same news programme, it is quite likely there may be another sort of queue on view – the queue for bread in one of the many danger zones of our world – a refugee camp in Darfur, perhaps, or Northern Uganda where more than a million Acholi people have been forced from their land, and rely on the UN for their security, and charities for their food. See the children holding their bowls out for a meagre portion of rice; follow the father humping back a sack of flour that must feed six mouths for a month. Try to remember when you last felt that hungry.

Consider what this Gospel would say to the people in the first queue, and consider if it could make sense to the people in the second. What does Jesus really mean here? We know he is not a puritan who insisted on fasting for its own sake. Think how many times he is depicted at a meal, and how often he spoke of the kingdom as a banquet. But neither was he a hedonist. He is not saying 'live for today' when he says 'each day has enough trouble of its own'. He is not telling us to go about naked, but that our beauty should be evident in many ways and not rely on silk and satins. So what should be the proper Christian attitude to food and display and security?

A clue lies in the position of this passage within Matthew's recording of the Sermon on the Mount. Jesus has taken the three traditional observances of Judaism – almsgiving, prayer and fasting, and opened up their reality for everyone. Just a few verses earlier, he has taught us how to pray: 'Give us today our daily bread'. So the Gospel we are reading this week is a gloss on that line.

Consider the difference between short-term and long-term planning and action. Jesus would expect us to look to the long term in dealing with climate change and peacemaking, both of which are vital if we are to feed all the abandoned people of the world. But he expects us to act now: today. We must not be paralysed by fear of the future.

In this reading we have reached the last of this group of gospel readings taken from the Sermon on the Mount. Consider, if all the other words of Jesus had been lost, and all that had been saved was the Sermon on the Mount, we would have all we need to teach us the radical lifestyle a Christian is expected to lead.

Contemplate your anxieties and troubles; contemplate the worries that plague you in the middle of the night. Bring them out into the light of day where the birds fly and the lilies grow.

Will worrying about them bring in the kingdom?

Will dwelling on them lead to righteousness?

As you desire to imitate him

Dear Jesus, help me distinguish between my needs and my wants.

Help me make your kingdom my priority

And your righteousness my goal.

Then with serenity I will look forward to tomorrow.

Amen.

The Sunday next before Lent

Matthew 17.1–9

Gaze on the barren summit of a windswept mountain. See the three disciples, Peter, James and John, cowering with fear, wishing there was a cave or even a tree where they could run and hide. First of all they've been blinded by a great light that seemed to consume Jesus; then they were astonished by the appearance of Elijah and Moses. When their terror had subsided a little, suddenly the sky lost its normal vivid blue and a cloud swept across blotting out the sun, yet radiating its own brilliance. Finally the voice of God boomed out from above them. No wonder they are terrified this must be the end of the world. There they kneel – grovelling, faces buried in their hands, making themselves as small as possible, aware of their utter insignificance. '*But* Jesus came and touched them.' Feel the warmth and reassurance of that touch and hear the gentle command in his voice: 'Do not be afraid.' Their heart rate subsides, their breathing calms, and they dare to look up again. Watch as they rise to their feet at last and gaze again on Jesus.

Consider why these events took place on a mountain top. Just as Moses received the Ten Commandments from God on Mt Sinai, so we have to step aside from the daily grind and distractions to step into God's presence. We need a better view.

Consider where we have heard the words 'this is my Son, my Beloved', before. Only a few weeks ago, at Christ's baptism in the Jordan, God revealed Jesus in full glory for just a moment. There, at the beginning of Jesus' ministry, God was signalling his approval of everything Jesus would go on to achieve. And now, as we enter Lent and the terror of the Passion, God seals his relationship in the same manner and with the same words.

Consider how imperfect the disciples were and yet how privileged to share this vision of Christ. Lent is partly for this – to help us stride or stumble towards a holier life, to open our eyes to God's forgiving grace and his cleansing judgement. The season of Lent is the opportunity the Church provides for us to grow closer to God so that we too may share the disclosure of Jesus in his glory.

This story concentrates on how the disciples reacted to the Transfiguration. But take a moment to consider what Jesus' own reaction might have been. Would he have been surprised, reluctant, or would he have understood what God was revealing in this moment?

Contemplate how transitory are the moments of glory in our lives. Yet they burn in the memory and remain beacons that see us through the trudging days on the plain and the tragic times in the valley.

Contemplate one moment of beauty that you remember. How did it speak to you of God?

As you desire to imitate him

Transfigured Lord, grant me
Moments when I may glimpse your glory
And hear the voice of God.
As I prepare to enter Lent
On my knees in penitence,
Touch me with your powerful love
And give me the strength once more
To stand upright in your presence.
Amen.

LENT

The First Sunday of Lent

Matthew 4.1–11

Gaze on the view from the top of a cathedral or a castle keep. You've climbed hundreds of worn, stone steps, twisting round the narrow internal staircase with only a narrow slit to let in light, and your heart is racing. At last you feel the breeze and see the light ahead as you come out onto the parapet. If you are lucky, there are sturdy railings all around. The view below is a maze of streets and, in the distance, a chessboard of fields; the sheep and cattle are like animals in a children's toy farmyard. Villages and towns are dimly visible on the horizon. You lean over the edge of the parapet, and experience the fear of falling.

Consider the difference between the verbs testing and tempting. Think about the tests you've had in your life. Tests at school to see how much you've learnt; tests in hospital, to find out the cause of illness, or maybe the exciting test to discover if a baby is on the way. Consider the way athletes test themselves, always pushing further and harder, determined to improve. Such testing has a place in all our lives, to keep us from complacency. Tests measure us up against a standard, and give us a goal to strive towards. It is to be expected that God will test us. We learn about that in the Old Testament.

But temptation does not come from God. Temptation always comes from the devil. The objects of the temptation are always very attractive, and sometimes very insignificant: another hour in bed, another bottle of wine, where's the harm? But if we give way to the little things, how will we cope when faced with a larger challenge? Succumbing to temptation, even the smallest, in some sense chips away at the integrity of our self. It either harms our ability to respond to God, or harms others.

Consider the links between Jesus' forty days in the desert, before the angels came and attended him, and the forty years of the tribes of Israel, wandering the wilderness before they found the promised land. The people were often tested, and at other times were tempted to disobey the will of their God. And when they gave in to temptation, they faced disaster.

The Old and the New Testaments are always in dialogue with each other, and we should use the Old Testament to illuminate the message of the New, and the New to correct the Old.

Contemplate the devil's third temptation, the worst of them all: 'bow down and worship me.'

Contemplate how often the temptations we struggle with are disguised versions of this enticement, which is to give up on God and turn towards the world. For our faith is hard and sometimes there seems little reward. We see others lead easier lives, and begin to wonder if there is much point in trusting in God rather than the ways of the world.

Contemplate the decisions you've made recently and the choices you need to make soon. Whom will they prove you to be worshipping?

As you desire to imitate him

Dear Lord, when I am tested may I grow through the experience
And strengthen my resolve to follow you.
When I am tempted, help me to resist
The enticements that lead away from you
And would keep me forever wandering in the wilderness.
Amen.

The Second Sunday of Lent

John 3.1–17

Gaze on Nicodemus, sitting alone one day in his comfortable home, mulling over the conversation he'd overheard Jesus have in the Temple. He's picturing in his mind the wonderful healings he's seen, too, and knows these are the signs of more than just a good man. But Jesus' behaviour doesn't fit into the strict pattern that a Pharisee would expect, and he's confused.

Watch Nicodemus walk quickly to the house where Jesus is staying. See him pull his cloak around himself at the unexpected wind that begins to blow. Imagine him hesitate, pace up and down two, three, four times, nerving himself to enter.

Something in the pit of his stomach tells him what he's about to do is momentous. By crossing this threshold, he'll step over from a world where everything makes sense to a new beginning where the rule book he grew up with, and had been part of upholding, has been torn up. No wonder his hand trembles as he opens the door and peers in.

Consider why this reading appears not only in Year A, but in Year B of our Lectionary cycle. In Year B we'll hear this reading for Trinity Sunday, when it will focus on the threefold nature of God which Jesus expounds in it.

But now it is Lent, and it is in John's company that we will walk to Easter. Part of the purpose of Lent is to struggle to be born again 'from above' – in other words, through God's grace and not through our own controlling activity. Who knows when the precise moment of childbirth will come? The mother waits for the first contractions, the family and friends wait for the phone call, but no one can predict or plan. The baby is at the mercy of the mother, who is at the mercy of her body and its hormones which, like the wind blowing where she chooses, decide on the moment the muscles begin to push and the baby will descend the birth canal and be expelled into the world. The birth of the Spirit may be as painful and shocking as this.

The birth of the flesh only happens to us once in our lives, and we never remember it. But consider, have you ever reached a point in your life when you've had to make a major change – perhaps to overturn a long cherished belief, leave behind a safe career, or taken on a scary ministry in the Church? How does it feel when the solid ground falls away?

Consider the lives of the saints, like St Francis, who left his merchant family, rejected his father, and went out into the unknown, born again for the love of Jesus.

Contemplate the words: 'God so loved ... that he gave ...' (v. 16). Repeat them, over and over again.

Contemplate where signs of God's love through God's self-giving are visible in your life and community today. Look at where there is struggle, for that is where we may find the inspiration of the Spirit.

As you desire to imitate him

Father, give me the courage of Nicodemus:
When I ask 'How can this be?'
May I trust your answers and grasp the truth
And open myself to the risk of change,
Through the power of the Holy Spirit.
Amen.

The Third Sunday of Lent

John 4.5–42

Gaze on Jesus, tired and in need of a rest. And more than that, he's terribly thirsty. The dust is catching his throat, clinging to his eyebrows and caking his lips. Seldom in the Gospels do we see people coming to help Jesus. He who spent all his time in the service of others, must have longed for people to show him care, help, or a word of encouragement. And so, this time, he asks for water. At first the woman doesn't seem willing to help, though it's such a simple and important request. Was Jesus to be denied even this small comfort?

Consider Jesus crossing the gulf between people who have ancient differences. He's not too proud to seek a favour from a Samaritan, not afraid that he'll be tainted by contact or communion with her. He's willing to 'share a vessel' – pass a cup, with someone with whom he was not in total agreement on all things, some of them very important. Consider what this tells us about our sorry Christian disunity, and Jesus' priorities of inclusiveness and humility. He casts aside the barriers that we erect. What does it matter if we worship God on a mountain or in a temple, or with an organ or a guitar?

Consider the humility that Jesus expects of us, a humility that does not cling to a badge or insist that only one label contains the truth. Consider the breadth of this message: the Spirit of God is too great to be limited to a city or a mountain, a temple or a cathedral. Last week Nicodemus was warned of the Spirit's freedom, and this week we hear the same.

Nor is Jesus too proud to discuss theology with a woman. Nor does he exclude her because of her dubious virtue. If Jesus excluded everyone who falls short in some way or another, who would have been left for him to debate with? Jesus is not threatened by controversy so he is free to see what is tradition and what is dogma and where these matter in our understanding of God. Tradition and dogma don't tell the whole truth, and both give an incomplete picture of God's plan. So he accepts the woman's right of access to God, as much of that of the pure living among us. Jesus would not flinch from a church where gay and lesbian people were welcome. He would not exclude them from his discourse.

Contemplate a situation in your life where groups have drawn boundaries and glare at each other with suspicion. It may be in the staffroom or the family or the local parish council. Contemplate God's Spirit washing away suspicion and God's truth illuminating our common humanity. Contemplate stepping across the perimeter into another's space, and contemplate the view from where they stand.

Contemplate Jesus speaking to you, despite your unworthiness. In the place of the woman's five husbands, recognize your five failings – list them, and name them now.

Contemplate him pouring over us the cleansing waters that bring eternal life and wash away our shames and sorrows.

As you desire to imitate him

Source of eternal life,
I thank you for the countless times
You quench my thirst. I thank you
For the waters turned to wine in Cana,
For the living water drawn from the well at Sychar,
For the water from your side on Calvary.
You offer me this water free of charge;
May I never thirst again.
Amen.

The Fourth Sunday of Lent

---◆◆◆◆---

John 9.1–41

Gaze on this as a drama in three acts. First, imagine the bare stage, set in some ordinary side street, where Jesus and his disciples enter from the wings. From the other side, we see the blind man enter, groping his way along, using a stick or his outstretched hands to check for obstacles ahead. He cannot see Jesus and must rely on his touch and his voice to decide if he can trust this person. Picture the neighbours congregating, as eager for answers as the disciples.

The next act is set inside the synagogue. It is dim in here, as dim as the thoughts of these leaders who can't see what's right in front of them. There follows an investigation, almost a trial – a practice run for that other trial that will all too soon take place. Though the arguments are all about Jesus, he himself is absent. Jesus is most often to be found out in the open, away from the secrecy of rooms.

Act three is out in the clear open air again, away from the shadows of intrigue and suspicion and vested interests. Here are the man and Jesus again, face to face. A few curious Pharisees trickle onto stage. But those with closed minds and closed eyes stay behind closed doors.

Consider the first question the disciples want answered, the one we all face in life some time or other: why do bad things happen to good people? For centuries before Jesus, and centuries after, our superstitious natures have found it easiest to believe disaster is caused by sin; that the person wasn't good after all, and deserves their fate.

Jesus opens the eyes not only of the blind man, but of the disciples, to the fact this is too simple and harsh a belief.

Consider this as a courtroom scene and yourselves as the jury. How would you weigh up the evidence about the healing? What proof would you look for? How difficult it is to start with an open mind, and not to bring to the case your own prejudices and upbringing. Do you trust the witness statements of strangers? The rational weighing of fact and theory is important, but first-hand evidence is always the best – 'One thing I do know. I was blind but now I see!' (v. 25).

A wise decision must surely unite your head and your heart. Then you can be confident you've reached a conclusion you can live by.

Consider how near in our reading we are to the final crisis of Jesus' life. All the ingredients of Jesus' final trial are here. This controversy has come about because of the threefold challenge of Jesus to the leaders as guardians of the truth: by curing the blind man in the first place and declaring it 'the work of God' (v. 3); second, by doing it on the Sabbath he once more threatens the status quo; and, third, by his accusation that these leaders are themselves the ones who are blind.

It is as if this is a rehearsal for Good Friday.

Contemplate blindness. Shut your own eyes and contemplate the darkness for a while. Try to walk and not to stumble.

Contemplate how damning Jesus' words are to all of us who refuse to really see. The guilt that the leaders try to place on the blind man is their guilt, not his. For Jesus turns the whole story upside down. Where it started with a blind beggar, it ends with the blindness of the leaders, who are not prepared to look at the truth of God with open eyes.

As you desire to imitate him

Jesus, Lord and Healer,
When I cling to false beliefs
Give me spiritual insight.
Put aside my obstinacy of thought
So that I can see clearly.
May I look through your eyes
And know that all are deserving,
And none are beyond your healing powers.
Amen.

The Fifth Sunday of Lent

John 11.1–45

Gaze on a deathbed. Often today this is in hospital, a curtained bed where relatives huddle and whisper; other people avert their eyes when they pass by, afraid to intrude. Watch while the loved one's breath ebbs away. Listen to the effort of the lungs, gasping for air. The person's face is etched with the pain of breathing, their skin pallid and their eyes dull. These eyes look beyond you; you do not see what it is they are gazing at. You tell them of your love, hoping that they can still hear you. Watch their expression change as the life flows from them and the frown of concentration smoothes at last. Their hand in yours brings comfort to you both. You can't share the journey they are about to embark on, and you do not know where they have gone. A body still lies in front of you, but where is the person?

Consider how very real death is. We must not diminish the reality of death.

That is why Jesus grieved, and why he wept. Consider all the strangers Jesus had healed; yet the person closest to him dies without him. He appears to have failed Lazarus and his sisters in their greatest need. The onlookers don't miss the irony of this: why didn't he help here, when he helped so many before? (see v. 37). Mary and Martha thought the same – 'Lord, if you had been here'.

Consider all the 'if onlys' of your life. If only you hadn't been flustered by that last-minute phone call, you wouldn't have locked yourself out of the house; you'd have passed that exam 'if only' they'd asked the questions you'd revised for; that crash would never have happened 'if only' you'd taken another route to work that day.

Our lives are so contingent on random events. Things may or may not occur in the way we prefer, and so many events are fortuitous. Mere chance seems to govern so much. Can we distinguish between coincidence and the hand of God? For Jesus drew his power from the unchanging God, and through him, the chance happenings of our existence are made sense of.

Consider the difference between the raising of Lazarus and the rising of Jesus. Lazarus was resuscitated and unchanged, the same man and brother that he'd always been. Though in his heart he must have been altered by this miracle, he continued his life within the same limits of humanity. The rising of Jesus, on the other hand, which we call his resurrection, transformed him into the divine Christ, and a new being. The raising of Lazarus was less for his sake than for Martha's, to show her that living within the love of Christ is a risen life.

Contemplate the difference between immortality, which the world strives for, and resurrection, which Jesus offers us.

We know our loved ones will not return as Lazarus did, but we place them in the everlasting arms of the Father, trusting that when his plan for the universe is fulfilled, they will be transformed.

As you desire to imitate him

Risen Lord, through your healing and godly power
You restored people to life.
I cannot imagine what resurrection will mean for myself
Or those I have loved.
But when I come to leave this world
May I trust my body to your care
And enter into your glory.
Amen.

Palm Sunday
The Liturgy of the Palms

Matthew 21.1–11

Gaze on the old city of Jerusalem, the narrow lanes choked with shoppers and craftsmen and crowded with pilgrims. Walk past the noisy blacksmiths' quarter, and wander through the district where they dye cloth, and the brilliant emerald and aquamarine hang out to dry like banners. All comers are pressed together, the rich jostle with the poor, in a jumble of humanity. Smell the spices on the stalls, see the dates piled up high in shining heaps, and the oranges glowing in the streets so narrow the sun hardly reaches them.

Listen to the hubbub as Jesus and the disciples enter into these dark and cobbled streets and the hooves of the colt clatter on the stones. The shouts of the street sellers fall quiet. The beggars stand and stare, surprised at this faintly ridiculous sight of the man on the donkey, only a little higher than the crowd, just a bit above eye level. So he could easily catch your eye, and recognize you.

Consider the crowd that Matthew describes – a 'very large crowd', he writes. From now on in the Passion story the crowd becomes one of the central characters in this drama. They are not a walk-on part to be acted by extras, they will be a leading contributor to the story. And we are all members of that crowd.

Consider the power of crowds and the danger that they turn into a mob. For once people turn over control of their minds and wills to the crowd, they can be swayed to act quite against their better judgement. This is not the only crowd in history to turn its back on the just.

But today, the crowd is fired up (consider how we use that word 'fired', consider the danger of flames), in eagerness for the challenge that Jesus' very entry to the Holy City is making to the authorities. What did they really consider his mission was?

Consider the word 'Hosanna'. We use it carelessly, treating it as an exotic alternative to 'Hurray'. But originally it meant 'Save us'. This was therefore a prayer and a proclamation combined. 'Save us, Son of David,' was in effect as good as proclaiming Jesus as Messiah.

Consider, what did they want saving from? This crowd was made up of the sick who wanted saving from illness, and the uncleanliness and exclusion that this incurred. There in the crowd were the poor who suffered under the joint load of Roman and Temple taxes, so that they could not feed their families. And there in the crowd too were young hotheads who believed that if only the Romans were kicked out of Judaea, the nation would thrive. Jesus appeared to be the answer to all these varied hopes and fears. He was the leader who would banish all their tribulations.

Contemplate Jesus approaching your college or factory or office, your church or chapel or club, your town, village or street. Will the police let him come, or issue an order preventing the march as a disturbance of the peace?

Contemplate calling out to him 'Save us, Lord!' What is it you mean by these words? What do you think is the worst blemish on our society today, the most dreadful threat it faces, or its most terrifying fear? Contemplate Jesus as saviour of the world as well as your personal redeemer.

As you desire to imitate him

Saving Lord Jesus, be with me at the crossroads of my life
When I can choose to go out into the unknown
Or retreat to comfort and security.
Help me trust in your power
Which is stronger than fickle excitement,
And believe in your word
Which lasts longer than the roar of the crowd.
Amen.

EASTER

Easter Day

————◆•◆•◆————

Matthew 28.1–10

Gaze as the women come over the brow of the hill. In the early morning shadows, everything looks bland and blank, bleached of colour. Smell the dewy earth, feel the hem of their skirts damp and smeared with dust. The rocky hillside is strewn with boulders and it's difficult to pick out which is Jesus' tomb. The women had fled that evening two days ago, chased away by the guards, so they'd left no sign to memorize it by. But as they approach their eyes grow accustomed to the half-light, and they remember it was over there, by that fallen tree stump. It was, wasn't it? Their disorientation is complete when they get nearer – are they wrong after all? They know acutely what it is to live in a world where nothing is certain, nothing predictable.

Consider all the extraordinariness of this description. Matthew has the worst of natural events – earthquakes – and the glory of angels, both playing a role in the resurrection. Is this earthquake the same that shook the Temple at the hour of Jesus' death (Matthew 27.51)? But if we look at it another way, how could an event that shattered the laws of nature not have occurred without such heralds? How could the miracle not take place without angels to bring his body back safely from the dead? Angels were the tireless deputies of God who had accompanied Jesus since his birth – there at the annunciation, the nativity, his baptism, his temptations, and his transfiguration. They were certainly not going to miss his resurrection, were they?

So we have earthquakes and angels and ordinary scared women – all things visible and invisible, as we recite in the creed. His death was the most public humiliation and torture. But his resurrection took place alone, none of his loved ones near, and we can only greet each other on Easter Sunday morning with the words 'He is risen', believing that between going to bed on Saturday night and waking on Sunday morning, the world has been turned upside down. The resurrection is the most invisible of God's actions, but Jesus became visible again – 'Greetings,' he said. 'Do not be afraid.'

Contemplate how, on Easter Day, the women endured extreme emotions, 'afraid yet filled with joy'. In the resurrection we experience both the fear of earthquakes – the world turned upside down – and the joy of angels, announcing good news. God is holding in one hand all the evil of the world and taking it from us, and in his other open hand he is offering all his love.

As you desire to imitate him

Crucified Christ, I did not see you rise,
   But you cast out my fears.
Risen Christ, I did not see the empty tomb,
   But you fill me with eternal life.
Eternal Christ, through whom I am made joyful,
   I give you thanks that you are Lord
Of all things, seen and unseen.
Amen.

The Second Sunday of Easter

John 20.19–31

Gaze on the doors of the house – note the plural. First there is the heavy external door, the main protection for the property, made of solid wood with massive hinges, and then another at the top of the stairs behind which the disciples cower. The bolts are still drawn across, but somehow proved useless. Gaze on the keys in the lock, the catch still engaged, but overcome.

Gaze on God's creation: there were no keys in Eden. There are no keys in the woods and fields, none in the mountains or rivers. Water flows freely, animals graze at liberty in the wild. It is only humans that keep cattle behind barbed wire and dam up the water and imprison their enemy.

Consider the place of keys in this world. They belong with motives of division and exclusion. They are part of a world where everything is labelled 'MINE' and 'KEEP OUT'. Think of the vain efforts we make in order to feel safe: the CCTV cameras, burglar alarms, padlocked gates, security codes and pin numbers we accumulate. Yet still we are burgled! Consider the costs of feeling safe. Consider what it is we seek to preserve or hang on to, how transitory it all is, how it will fade or turn to mould or disintegrate. All those treasures locked in the shed or basement or loft, we return to years later and wonder why ever we kept them. Time gives perspective and distance changes priority but we never learn how to be free. God's plan is for a world without barriers, where we can pass unchallenged. Consider what this really means – it is not for us to choose who will be allowed into heaven.

The resurrection is the beginning of a world without keys. Consider the day that Jesus lay trapped in his tomb. He took with him the

huge, clanking, rusting ring that held the keys of corruption, preju-
dice and greed down into hell. He threw them into the abyss and
left them there. So now, wherever God's power is allowed free range,
doors open regardless of bolts and bars.

Consider what doors your church should be unlocking in the parish
today, so that God's kingdom can reign.

Contemplate today's world, a prison with high walls built out of
cynicism, hypocrisy and lack of love. Contemplate in which way
you've locked yourself in. Consider who you've locked out.

Contemplate inviting Jesus to come into your private home and
be with you there. Find the courage to open the door and welcome
the stranger who waits outside – the hooded teenager, the immigrant
whose accent you can't understand, the person with mental health
problems desperate for real 'care in the community'.

As you desire to imitate him

Risen Lord, help me throw away the keys
That lock me into a divided world.
As my fears are my chains, so I pray for trust;
As my selfishness is my jailer, so I pray for charity;
As my pride is the bolted door, so I pray for humility.
For by your resurrection, the imprisonment of sin has been abolished.
Amen.

The Third Sunday of Easter

Luke 24.13–35

Gaze in your memory on the many times in your life you've met with a stranger. Remember the anxious feelings – the butterflies in your stomach, or the fear of embarrassment. You go to a new school, where you don't know a soul; you join a football team or hockey club, or painting class, and don't recognize anyone. A new member of staff starts at the office, or a new neighbour moves into your road, or a new vicar comes to the parish. How do you begin to get to know them? You are introduced to a friend of a friend – you smell their aftershave or perfume, you either like it, or it puts you off. The person sitting next to you on the train starts chatting, and you notice the book they are reading. What makes you want to know them better? Is it the way they're dressed or their words or their eyes? Slowly you decide whether this is a person you can trust. In the same way Cleopas and the other disciple came to feel at ease with this stranger, and learned to trust him as they walked along together.

Consider how actions speak louder than words. Jesus wore himself out talking to the disciples. Yet here he is again, patient as ever, 'beginning with Moses and all the Prophets' (v. 27). How long must this lecture have taken him as they trudged along to Emmaus!

Consider how the disciples were still confused by Jesus' real purposes: 'We had hoped that he was the one who was going to redeem Israel' (v. 21). They wanted a strong leader who would restore Israel's independence but his death had ended that dream.

Consider how each disciple in his or her own way had to come to terms with this disillusion.

And one by one they came, in their own time, to realize that Jesus' work in the world was aimed at a replacement of all worldly power.

He had not come to wield just another version of such power. His death and resurrection ushered in a radical re-ordering of personal and social relationships between individuals and with God which, if fully adopted, would dispense with the tyranny of power altogether.

Consider how Jesus doesn't accuse these two of being dull witted or lazy thinkers. Instead, he tells them off for being 'slow of heart' (v. 25). So when Cleopas and his friend finally recognize their Lord, they say 'were not our hearts burning within us?' (v. 32). The recognition of Jesus as our Lord requires a physical response. Belief is more than intellectual assent.

Consider what these men then did. 'They got up and returned at once to Jerusalem' (v. 33), their fear transformed into courage. Belief in the resurrected Christ demands of us a turning around which leads to brave decisions and determined action.

Contemplate how Jesus was made known in the action of the breaking of the bread.

Contemplate how you make Jesus known to others – through the hospitality of a shared meal, through building up another's sense of worth, by listening to them, through sacrificing your time or your pleasure for their needs; through a wise word or generous gesture.

As you desire to imitate him

Companion Jesus, walk with me when I journey
And stay with me when I come to rest.
May my heart burn within me when we meet
And then may I be ready to take the next step
Towards your will for me.
Amen.

The Fourth Sunday of Easter

---•◆•---

John 10.1–10

Gaze or, this time, listen. Listen to a person's voice and wonder what it is about the timbre that makes it recognizable. Each voice has a trace as unique as a fingerprint. Voices do not age in the same way as our faces do. Listen to the voice of a parent singing a lullaby, or the cheerful voice of a friend, or the powerful voice of a preacher. Listen to a voice trembling with sadness or a voice whispering of love or screaming abuse or curses. What makes a voice sound trustworthy? You will think twice before you follow a stranger's voice. What would Jesus' voice have sounded like? In this passage it would have sounded firm and determined.

Consider how Jesus is apparently opening up these hard and deep truths to 'the Jews' – a wider audience than the disciples, and yet he does not patronize his listeners. Consider today's world of multiple choices. Our consumer culture has permeated even our religious thinking. We are dishonest to ourselves and to God if we think we can 'pick and mix' our beliefs. The Church should not be ashamed to say who it is that we follow. Jesus says the sheep pen only has one gate, which is he himself. And next week's Gospel will underline this, when we read 'I am the way and the truth and the life' (John 14.1–14).

These sayings trouble many people, for how do we reconcile the harshness of the claim in v. 9, 'whoever enters through me will be saved', with the inclusive nature of Jesus' love which shines throughout the Gospels?

Part of the answer may lie in the verses we would read if we continued just beyond this morning's Gospel. In v. 16, Jesus tells us, 'I have sheep that are not in this pen.' Jesus as a Jew was willing to embrace the Samaritan and the Roman. He did not insist they abandon their religion, or the ways of their forefathers, before he helped them; he did insist they recognize his truth in their lives. How do we know that Jesus is not in the hearts and faiths of these other people, helping them come to God too?

Contemplate the final verse of our Gospel and the times or moments in your life when you could say you lived life 'to the full'. When was it, and what were you doing, and who were you with? Why was it different from the ordinary existence of the daily round?

Contemplate the abundance of generosity experienced on your birthday, or the abundance of praise when you leave a job and colleagues make you feel so special. Contemplate the abundance of proper pride when you've run the marathon or passed exams. Contemplate the over-abundance of a parent's love, or the feeling of falling in love. These are mere glimpses of the abundance Jesus wills us to live in day by day.

As you desire to imitate him

Dear Shepherd, may I recognize your voice above the din of the world
And the clamour of my own desires.
Help me resist the tempter's beguiling voice
And follow you in safety through the gate
That leads to abundant life.
Amen.

The Fifth Sunday of Easter

John 14.1–14

Gaze on all the maps you use in daily life. On a trip to London, you stare at the maze of the Underground, trying to follow the snake-like threads of the different lines, and make sense of the colour codes. There's the A to Z of the local town, the index in such small print that only young eyes can decipher the street names. You look up the co-ordinates, G5 or X4 and still can't find the street you're hunting for. Gaze on a road map of a strange city you are entering for the first time – how do you know which are one-way streets? Even if you've taken the map off the web, it may not account for recent road works and the inevitable diversions. Of course, you may be lucky and have SatNav. People rely on this 'as gospel', certain it is 100 per cent accurate, until it lands them in a river, or a farmyard full of manure.

Consider how, like Thomas, we need every day to refer to some sort of map or instruction manual, even if it is only a recipe, to get by or find our way. As it is in daily life, so it is in our moral and spiritual life – we all need a compass.

It is natural, as we read these gospel excerpts week by week, that we concentrate our attention on Jesus as guide. It is his life we follow from cradle to grave and beyond. It is his preaching and parables we ruminate over. But sometimes we are in danger of treating Christ as if he is the total manifestation of God. We get confused, like Philip, when we think of Jesus as God. Is that all of God there is? Certainly not, for consider how much stress Jesus always laid on the fact that 'the words I say to you are not just my own' and 'it is the Father, living in me, who is doing his work' (v. 10).

64

Consider how this week's reading, and next week's which follows straight on, anticipate the great celebrations of Pentecost and Trinity which are just ahead of us. 'I am in the Father and the Father is in me', Jesus says, and he repeats it to make sure we've taken it in. He is trying to describe the unity at the heart of the Trinity, just as next week he continues with his promise of the Counsellor, so that the Trinity will be complete. We should not reserve thinking about the Trinity to one Sunday of the year, but be alert to the many times the threefold dimensions of God are necessary parts of our direction-finding kit.

Contemplate the face of Jesus, and see the Father in him. Hear the words of Jesus and know they are from God. Contemplate the work of Jesus, and see in it the actions of God. Do not be like a child in a game of blind man's buff, ever-circling and stumbling. Feel the rescuing hand of your mother on your shoulder, and trust that she will lead you in the right direction.

As you desire to imitate him

Jesus my guide, through whom I come to know the Father,
So strengthen my trust and confirm my faith
That I may walk through the mazes of my life
With an untroubled heart
And enter the place you have prepared for me.
Amen.

The Sixth Sunday of Easter

John 14.15–21

Gaze on a group of African children orphaned by HIV & AIDS, longing for that one person who will be special to them, and who will make them know they are loved above everyone else. As kind as the staff are, as supportive as the older children are, as loving as their siblings may be, these 'little ones' search for their parent, knowing that they have a hole in their heart that only Mum and Dad can fill.

Gaze on the young children in your family or known to you, and remember the panic behind their eyes when the babysitter arrives and you tell them you're going out. How do they know you'll ever return? Only as they grow older does their trust increase. Hear the parent say 'I won't ever leave you. I'll be back very soon.' That is the promise Jesus gives here, in verse 18.

Consider the interdependence of this Son and his Father, and us, his children – one moment the stress is on *you* will see me, *you* will live, *you* will realize. Then it reverses and the emphasis is *I am* in my Father, *I am* in you.

In this complicated web of promises and pronouns, not only does Jesus pledge the Counsellor – the Spirit of Truth – but he also promises his own return, and explains that on that day of return, the Jesus we meet will be inextricably – if inexplicably! – one with the Father. So we are looking ahead both to Pentecost and to Trinity Sunday.

Consider the Spirit of Truth: first, the truth about ourselves, the inescapable truth of our lostness and incompleteness. Second, the truth about the world: no power structures can provide security, no wealth can secure lasting happiness, and no medicine can prevent death. Third, the truth of Jesus, that his love and transforming forgiveness can cure the lostness, provide the security, bring healing between peoples and nations, and overcome death. It is these truths which make possible the promise that 'you also will live'.

Contemplate the gap between the promises made here, and their fulfilment. 'You will see me', Jesus promises – but when? A sense of waiting pervades this passage. Contemplate the waiting times of your life. You wait for exam results or a house purchase to be agreed, with anxiety and some excitement. You wait for a baby to be born or a lover to return, knowing that all things will be transformed by their arrival. Contemplate the virtue of patience.

As you desire to imitate him

Spirit of Truth, give me patience to wait for your coming.
Eternal Counsellor, ignite in me divine life,
Unite me with the Father,
Enable me to obey your commandments
And to know your love.
Amen.

The Seventh Sunday of Easter

John 17.1–11

Gaze on some of the earliest Christian paintings, the third-century frescos in the catacombs of Rome. On the wall of the catacomb of Priscilla is depicted a Christian worshipping God – standing upright with a prayer shawl over his (?) head, arms uplifted and outstretched. This posture suggests an openness to God, and a belief that one is welcome to look at him, and it is in this manner that Jesus would have prayed to his heavenly Father. The people of the New Testament saw the sky as full of angels and stars, of doves and the sound of voices, of God hidden in clouds. Look up to the sky and what do you see? By day, you are surrounded by three hundred and sixty degrees of space, stretching to infinity. Clouds may cluster and spread their shapes, forever shifting, or a warm haze may skim the blue. Birds fly freely till they disappear from view. By night, the stars draw you up into their impenetrable secret. The sky harbours the sun that brings us warmth and it is from the sky that life-giving rain comes. Thunder and lightening rule and terrify us. So, however much we try to leave behind our childish, pre-scientific understanding, the sky still fills us with awe, just as it did for Jesus when he prayed.

Consider the meaning we attach to ideas of ascension. Our senses, our minds and our cultures all combine to insist that height equals superiority. Here in this passage we start with the words 'glorify' and 'authority', to reinforce the idea of ascension, and relate it to triumph and victory. The collect for the day talks of the exalting of Jesus – the setting aloft, according to the dictionary definition. Jesus was friend, and is now king; was teacher and is now ruler; was brother and is now God. In some way, he has become more distant from us, removed from the ordinariness of everyday.

Consider how we talk about the 'heights' of emotion. We talk about putting people on a pedestal – think of Nelson on his column, for here we see a hero set far out of our reach. We talk of people reaching the 'high point' of their career, or being at the height of their physical fitness. The winner's podium is always higher than that of the runner up. A monarch ascends his or her throne, literally as well, for the throne is always raised on a dais. All these images assert their dominance by their height. But is this really what the Ascension of our Lord was about? Jesus' last words in this extract are 'that they may be one', which is hardly a concept of superiority, but much nearer the attitude of the praying man we gazed on above, unafraid to look God in the eyes.

Contemplate the order of events of the past few weeks – crucifixion followed by a waiting for the resurrection; resurrection followed by a waiting till the Ascension; Ascension followed by a waiting till the coming of the Holy Spirit. And soon, Pentecost, followed by a waiting – how long? – for the Second Coming. Each a complete gift in itself and yet incomplete until the next act of God. All our relationships are lived in this way, for true relationship is never static and we always hope for more.

Contemplate the phases of your Christian life and ask God to reveal the next gift he has in store for you.

As you desire to imitate him

Holy Father and Loving Son, I look for you in heaven
And I wait for you on earth.
Grant to all who accept your word
The joy of approaching you, now king but still friend,
Exalted and yet still brother to us all.
Amen.

Day of Pentecost

John 7.37–39

Gaze on a river in all its varied stages. At first it is a silent trickle, welling up from a spring, always replenished yet forever hidden. Then the quiet country stream brings delight to children who picnic by its bank and paddle in its shallows. But soon it picks up speed and tumbles over weirs and leaps down vertiginous waterfalls. Now it is in full spate, moving with such gusto and power that it cleanses the river bed, brings boulders along its path, cuts gorges through mountains, proving the strength of water over stone. In maturity it meanders through water meadows, looping across the landscape, glinting silver like the back of a bird, requiring huge bridges to allow us to cross. Finally, it reaches the estuary and yields to the sand, and joins the salt of the sea.

Consider why it is rare in the Gospels to get any description of Jesus, or any clue as to his appearance or demeanour. We certainly have no description of how he looked, except at the moment of the extraordinary transfiguration. Even the telling of his resurrection appearances omit any real description or what he looked like. And yet perhaps this is right; if we did have a picture of Jesus, that might make it harder for us to make room for the Spirit, or comprehend the Trinity.

What we do have here is itself unusual – a comment on how Jesus spoke: with a 'loud voice'. Why do people raise their voices? Sometimes to be heard over a crowd, or sometimes in anger. Often, it is to emphasize a point, as Peter and the disciples would have done in today's reading from Acts, passionate to convince the crowd of the importance to them all of what has just taken place. So passionate, in fact, that his words make sense to foreigners who normally couldn't understand Aramaic. How strange that the most important message of all was delivered in what might have appeared as chaos and confusion. Here, in the Gospel, Jesus is trying to convince others too, and so he pronounces his promise boldly. At other times of revelation in the Gospels, we've heard God's own voice, descending from the clouds. Now it is Jesus who declares the arrival of the Spirit. To help us understand, he compares it to 'streams of living water'.

Consider the stages of the river we looked at above, and examine where you are on your spiritual journey.

Contemplate the kind of water Jesus requires you to be at this particular stage of your life. We are not to be stagnant pools, or water dammed up in a reservoir. His Spirit is given to us to enable us to cascade over obstacles, and to be bubbling white water that rinses everything in its way. But if you are older, or unwell, or weary of service, contemplate stooping down to the cool clear water, and quenching your thirst.

As you desire to imitate him

God of many voices, but one Holy Spirit,
God of many languages but one true Word,
Speak to me loudly over the roar of the world.
Spirit of living water, flow through me,
Spirit of rushing wind, sweep me off my feet,
Spirit of flame, ignite my heart and will.
Spirit of God's breath, inspire me.
Amen.

ORDINARY TIME

Trinity Sunday

Matthew 28.16–20

Gaze for the last time on Jesus, for this is his final appearance in Matthew's Gospel, and the ending is sudden. No protracted goodbye is allowed for the disciples. There is no description of how they met him on the mountain top, and we must imagine it for ourselves. Just what had happened to Jesus – how does he look now? Is he peaceful, or troubled still? He must have changed somehow for the majority of them to have worshipped him, something they never did when he lived with them. Matthew uses the word 'worship' once before in this closing chapter, when the women meet Jesus after the resurrection. A Jew would never prostrate themselves to a ruler or a teacher. So what made them stretch out on the ground this time, before their friend? What new power or truth shone from his eyes?

Consider the muddle Matthew makes of our festivals. He's jumped over the Sundays after Easter by leaving out all of Jesus' post-resurrection appearances. He's combined Pentecost and the Ascension into one event. He is not setting out to give us a chronology or a catalogue of evidence. We must take or leave his resurrection account on the evidence of the angel and the women alone. So what was his intention?

In these last five verses, he opens up for us the mystery of the Trinity. Jesus is now placed at God's right hand with 'all authority'. He is reunited with the Father and the Spirit, and it is in the name of all three that the disciples must act.

This passage is usually known as 'The Great Commission' – 'therefore, go!' – for consider the list of actions that are imposed on us: to make disciples, to baptize and to teach, and to obey God's command-ments. Many of us strive to obey the last of this list, but how many of us make progress with the first three? Here in a nutshell is the imperative for mission. Here also is the Trinity. It is the Father we obey, it is the Son whose disciples we are, and it is the Spirit who baptizes. And our task is not just to individuals, it is to entire nations. Over the last 2,000 years we've made a good start on this, but in our modern age of global diversity and mutual respect, it is difficult to know how to complete this charge. We can only ask for the guidance of the Spirit as we learn to live with a variety of faiths and work for the kingdom with them, and not against them.

Contemplate Christ's last words, his great promise: 'And surely I am with you always, to the very end of the age.' The trauma of the farewell is reversed by this promise. We are not left alone to struggle with impossible challenges. With the order, comes the strength; with the challenge, comes the means.

As you desire to imitate him

Holy Trinity, Holy Unity,
I bow to your authority over my life.
I accept your commission
To make disciples.
I welcome the empowering Spirit
Into my life,
And I rely on your promise
To be with me always.
Amen.

Proper 4

————•◦•————

Matthew 7.21–29

Gaze on a building project near you. First the fencing goes up, then the site is levelled and all the rubble cleared away. Dust swirls around and covers your jeans. The land is surveyed and the plan pegged out. The rooms look so small ruled out on the ground. Then come the cranes and diggers, burrowing feet below the surface to make the footings, and all the waste is transported off site. Then the noisy concrete mixer gets going, pouring tons and tons into the foundations, making the base sturdy and steady. Now scaffolding is erected, and a vast framework appears within which the building will rise. Only then will the brick walls begin to appear. These days it might take almost a year to build such a house. Two thousand years ago, houses were smaller and simpler, but still the builder knew the importance of firm foundations.

Consider the difference between our epistle this week (Romans 1.16–17 and 3.22–28), and this Gospel. We are faced with a paradox, aren't we? Paul insists 'a man is justified by faith, apart from observing the law', and yet Jesus tells us only they who *do* the will of the Father will enter the kingdom. How can their views be so at odds? Which one is right? Are we to rely on faith then, or are we exhorted to act?

We should remember that Paul is very much a man of the Old Testament, which was full of prohibitions. It was that old, decaying law that he rejected, and Jesus' fresh freedom that he strove to teach. The Gospel, on the other hand, proclaims a living law which 'does the will' of the Father. So, in fact, Paul and the gospel writer are much closer together than at first sight. Jesus didn't want us to harp on about how compliant we are, or make a lot of fuss about how we are fully paid up members. Even to prophesy and heal may not be

76

sufficient, if we have not lived within the spirit of the Sermon on the Mount (of which this is the conclusion). We may listen and pray with conviction on Sunday, yet speed carelessly on Monday, fiddle our expenses on Tuesday, shout at our partner on Wednesday, gossip about the Rector on Thursday, and harden our heart by Friday. And all the time we behave this way, we are so disguising our discipleship that eventually Jesus is forced to say 'I never knew you.'

Contemplate how firm the foundations of your faith are. What is your trust built on? Is it built on wishful thinking, or serious reading of the Bible? Is it built on dreams or prayer? Is it built on personal assumptions or shared teaching? Contemplate how tall buildings are designed to sway a little in the wind – if they don't, they'll break. Is your faith too rigid to withstand the floods and gales that being human means you'll surely have to face one day?

As you desire to imitate him

Jesus, I will build my life on your foundations
And dare to call you Lord.
When storms brew may my faith stand firm.
Though often tired and tempted
May I do the will of your Father,
So that you need never reject me.
Amen.

Proper 5

Matthew 9.9–13, 18–26

Gaze on Matthew, sitting in his tax booth. He's snappily dressed in the latest trend, looks like a city trader with designer shades hiding his eyes, a wide tie round his neck; a striped suit and Italian leather shoes complete the outfit. Round his wrist is a Rolex watch that might be real, but is probably fake. His whole appearance is designed to brag about his success. In his hand is the latest phone so that he's never out of contact with Herod's flunkies, and only one button away from harassing his 'customers'. His chin juts out in defiance as the crowd approach. He's fed up with being criticized. It may be a messy job, but life's messy, isn't it, and someone's got to do it. 'Better me than that rogue Benjamin,' he thinks, for he'd extort even more. But the dark glasses aren't just against the sun – Matthew finds it hard to look others in the eyes, and doesn't even like to look at himself too closely as he shaves each morning in the mirror.

Consider what Jesus saw in Matthew's hidden eyes. Consider why it took so little on this occasion for Matthew to leave his dubious life and follow Jesus – he must have already been feeling desperately in need of rescue. And when he heard Jesus criticize the Pharisees, those superior Jews who looked down their noses at the likes of him, he must have felt the first stirrings of understanding. He understood Jesus because Jesus understood – and accepted him.

Consider why this story is put besides two healing miracles, and what they have in common. The other two appear different at first sight, for they are about a physical healing. So it is worth asking, in what way did Matthew need healing? Alternatively we can ask whether the ruler would have considered himself a sinner. Jesus, in common with the accepted thought of his times, did not see such a great distinction between sickness and sinfulness, and so he easily extended his explanation, 'I have not come to call the righteous, but sinners' (v. 13), to them all.

Consider how good we are at self justification, just like Matthew. He must have battled daily to convince himself he was doing the right things. But the thing that binds these three stories together is that none of the characters – tax collector, ruler, or outcast woman – gained healing or deliverance by their own merits. Jesus spells it out to the woman: 'Your faith has healed you.'

Contemplate the words Jesus presses on us: 'I desire mercy and not sacrifice' (Hosea 6.6). It is the mercy of Jesus that saves, not sacrifice or ritual behaviour of our own. Last week we heard about our 'responsibility' for our salvation; this week we learn that even so, we must rely on God's action, his mercy. Contemplate this mercy, and learn what it means for you today. What activity or misunderstanding are you caught by, that Jesus is calling you away from?

As you desire to imitate him

Lord Jesus, too easily I divide the world
Between the deserving and the undeserving.
May I respond to people according to their needs
And not their righteousness,
And love people for their weaknesses,
Resting my faith on your mercy
Poured out to all sinners.
Amen.

Proper 6

Matthew 9.35—10.8

Gaze on the harassed and helpless, the dislocated and forgotten of our societies – like commuters without a train, milling around on the platform, tired after a long day standing on their feet serving in a shop for not much more than the minimum wage, longing to get home for a refreshing shower, a warm meal and the pleasure of their family. But a signal failure has stopped all the trains, and they must wait, how long they do not know, without much hope. They study the display board praying that it will announce their train, but all it says is 'delayed'. They long for an announcement that will say all has been put right.

Consider the meaning of the word *compassion*. It is made up of 'com', meaning 'with', and 'passion' – which derives from the Latin 'to suffer'. The dictionary definition is 'a pity inclining one to help or be merciful'. It is important we take note of the whole of this definition. Jesus did not just pity – he helped. We never read a gospel story that says 'Jesus met a beggar and said "What a pity", before walking by'; or 'they brought a sick woman to Jesus and he wished her better'. His heart was softened by the other's pain, and therefore he healed all who came to him. This Gospel, and last week's, continue to show how Jesus cured 'every disease and every sickness' because of his compassion. But the importance of this Gospel is that after the long list of healing and miracles, Jesus now insists that with compassion comes responsibility, for we must be sent out as the disciples to deliver the prescription for the cure. Another way of looking at it is that we must become the bridge over which Jesus' mercy can reach them.

But this is not a toll bridge which the needy must pay to cross. If we act with compassion, we act without expectation of any return or reward for ourselves. And Jesus reminds us why this must be: 'freely you have received, freely give' (v. 8). True compassion does not count the cost, but acts spontaneously through love for the other.

Contemplate God's compassion for us, for 'while we were still sinners, Christ died for us' (from today's epistle, Romans 5.8). This was giving without counting the cost, taken to extremes. Jesus laid himself down and became the bridge between our sinfulness and his Father's everlasting mercy. To quote a well-known song, he became a 'bridge over troubled water'.

As you desire to imitate him

Compassionate Father, though I suffer, I will persevere,
And through perseverance, my character will grow.
Shape me into readiness to work in your world,
To bring hope to the harassed and the helpless
Among those I will meet this week.
Amen.

Proper 7

———•◆•———

Matthew 10.24–39

Gaze on yourself in a mirror. If you are young, your face is open, unlined, your skin fresh and clear, and your eyes are bright. Whether you wear your hair long or cropped, bobbed or short, it is thick and glossy. Do you see the face of the child you have left behind? Can you predict what you will look like in thirty, forty, fifty years time?

If you are already older, you'll see the wrinkles of experience, frown marks on the forehead, or laughter lines around the eyes. Can you remember what you once looked like? Your hair may still be long, but whatever the colour, it's duller now. Blond has turned mousy, and dark is probably streaked with grey. You may already be silver, or bald. Even if not, you are used to the hair accumulating on your brush, and realize you are losing it faster than it grows. Who do you look like now? What will you look like at seventy, eighty, ninety – if you are spared? And you wonder, who is in charge of this process, for you know you are not.

Consider how we can reconcile the inevitability of ageing and decay with what Jesus is telling us: 'even the very hairs on your head are numbered, so do not be afraid.' We all ponder the randomness of nature. When we see a sparrow fallen from the nest, dead on the ground, or a fox run over in the road, we can't but ask ourselves, is this a wasted life? And even more, when we read heartbreaking tributes in the local paper to a two-year-old who's died of meningitis, we ask God where is the fairness or meaning in this, and how can this happen if he values us as much as he says?

Some Christians do believe that all is predestined and we are not to question the will of God, that our fate is determined and it is our duty to submit. Others query this, not understanding how it makes sense with our belief in free will, or with Jesus' desire that we live abundant lives. Whichever is nearer the mind of God, perhaps if we gazed at God more than ourselves, our fears would lessen. We cannot measure the value God places on each of us. And when this extract ends 'whoever loses his life for my sake will find it' we are reminded again that our worry about our survival is so misplaced.

Contemplate the stories in your life of loss, or threat or violence, for no one in their life is untouched by tragedy. And the temptation is always to ask 'Why me?' We can't answer that, but must learn to trust and wait on Jesus' promise that 'there is nothing concealed that will not be disclosed, or hidden that will not be made known' (v. 26).

As you desire to imitate him

Master and Teacher, it is hard to make sense of the tragedies of life.
I struggle to find meaning in the death of young children
Or to see your will in violence, conflict or famine.
Help me rest in your promise that though this earthly body fail,
It will be transformed.
Therefore, I will not be afraid.
Amen.

Proper 8

———◦•◦———

Matthew 10.40–42

Gaze on an old-fashioned prize-giving ceremony at the local school. First there are the prizes for best in French, or maths, or music. Then awards for the fastest runner or the highest jumper. Form prizes follow for the most helpful pupil, and recognition for prefects for their contribution to the smooth running of the school. Then come the special prizes – 'most improved of the year', or 'most sustained effort of the year' – prizes tailored so that not only the high achievers are noticed. Next come the odd prizes named after some obscure benefactor or illustrious old boy or girl. Each child trips up to the front, each parent swells with pride as the worthy book is handed out. Years later, the tome is discovered, dusty on a shelf, never read, and the inscription fading.

Is this the sort of reward Jesus has in store for us?

Consider this passage as a continuation of last week's teaching, which it concludes. And yet there is little at first glance to connect them. We move away from metaphysical reflections on the body and the soul, and away from warning of division, to a bold positive: 'He who receives you, receives me': those who go out in mission and are welcomed, are 'standing in' for Jesus, who in turn is 'standing in' for God, for both passages are part of Jesus' advice to the disciples whom he is sending out.

Consider the different forms that missionary activity can take today. Some people still give up everything to live and work in remote corners of the world, sacrificing comfort and success to 'stand in' for Jesus. Some work nearer to home, going into the poorer communities of our towns or counties, working with the hopeless and excluded. Some may teach in a tough comprehensive at the bottom of the league tables that will never win a reward or accolade. Others quietly 'stand in' for Jesus in their street, in loving service. Whether teaching or campaigning or praying, mission comes from God in the first instance and our particular 'activity' is our response to Christ. Our very identity should be a mark of mission. Then we will deserve recognition in Jesus' 'New Year's Honours List', according to our service.

Contemplate who are the 'little ones' in your life at the moment. Who are those in most need, who are most vulnerable or isolated? It might be someone you know who needs financial and practical support, but it could be someone who needs a word of support or the touch of love. Because you cannot solve their whole problem – heal the cancer, or restore a broken relationship – do not give up. Even 'a cup of cold water' might help.

As you desire to imitate him

Jesus, friend and leader, may I see your face
In the face of those you send me to,
And may I help them in the way
That only I am able,
Without concern for reward,
But with love overflowing,
Through your grace and in the power of the Spirit.
Amen.

Proper 9

—◦•◦—

Matthew 11.16–19, 25–30

Gaze on these children playing in the marketplace. Children are the same the whole world over, and in every era. Today they would be in the home corner, playing make-believe games. 'Let's play weddings,' says Kelly, who's recently been a bridesmaid at a family wedding. She grabs a piece of net curtain for her veil and waits for the bridal march to begin, and demands that Jake plays the groom. But he doesn't want to join in, and won't co-operate with her next choice either. It would be more unusual today to see children role-playing a funeral, but in Jesus' time these would have been much more public affairs and from a very young age children would have heard the high-pitched wail of the mourners, and might have tried to copy it. Hear Benjamin call out, 'You're not doing it right! You're spoiling the game!' Then off he goes, to sulk.

Consider why Jesus chose these examples. He must have despaired of the people who were convinced neither by John's wailing, nor by his own joy. While John preached with threats, Jesus preached with parties, but the onlookers accepted neither approach. Their confusion is all part of their inability to recognize 'wisdom proved right' (v. 19). Consider Jesus' attention to the idea of 'wisdom'. The concept of wisdom was highly prized by the Jews of that time, as it had been throughout their sacred writings. Wisdom was seen as the Law, or the heavenly mysteries, and part of the creation spirit. Of course we can also define it in our normal everyday sense. But whichever interpretation we choose, the shock here is that wisdom is revealed to children – the simple, the ignored, the barely literate.

Consider Jesus' final words here, his famous words of comfort. For despite our refusal to recognize him, he has an overwhelming care for us. He invited the weary to come to him – of what were they weary? Jesus is referring here mostly to the burden of always falling short. We so easily despair of living up to Jesus' standards. Jesus would also have been referring to the burden his contemporaries shouldered that most of us do not – the burden of onerous religious rules and laws that seemed to exclude all but the most virtuous from any chance of salvation. But the rest we are promised is not to be confused with idleness; it does come with a 'yoke' attached, by which Jesus means a discipline which gives a sense of direction.

Contemplate the difference between being complacent, being content, and being at rest. For true rest is neither complacent nor sometimes even content. The true rest that Jesus brings is being certain that we are working in his service, upheld with his love, and forgiven through his mercy. Such knowledge will surely fill us with energy.

As you desire to imitate him

I praise you, Father, Lord of heaven and earth,
Because you have made known your wisdom to the simple
And promise your rest to the weary.
I give you thanks, that through the Son, you are revealed
And I am invited to mirror your ways.
Amen.

Proper 10

Matthew 13.1–9, 18–23

Gaze on this field – it's easy to imagine, for Jesus has painted such a detailed picture. You may pass through such fields when you walk the dog. Together you stroll along the path, where in spring a few brave seeds have had the temerity to root. But the stones of the path and the tread of wellington boots soon batter them down. Gaze on the field in July: the sun comes out from behind a cloud, there is a light breeze and there before you stretch acres of summer wheat glowing gold and bending with grace and gratitude. Your dog chases away and is hidden by the height of the wheat, heavy with its crop. Around the field is a tough British hedge of hawthorn, holly and beech, all intertwined, smothered by brambles. Come autumn, you'll pick the succulent blackberries, but the farmer's seed has no chance here.

Consider why this is the first of Jesus' parables reported in Matthew. It is accessible and straightforward, easy to understand, and paints a picture any one can envisage. Some of his later parables are more complex, but for now Jesus is willing to be gentle with his listeners. Up till this moment in Matthew, Jesus has taught and healed, and only now does he turn to the 'many things in parables'. Perhaps that is why he is willing to elaborate and take the trouble to explain, whereas usually we must make the effort to understand. Indeed, his first retort was 'he who has ears, let him hear', but he softens and bends over backwards to help the disciples. Not that this parable needs much explanation. How easily we recognize ourselves as the one who lets worries or wealth choke them, or who gives up at the first obstacle. As it was once said, Christianity has not been tried and found wanting; it has been tried and found difficult.

But consider the crumb of comfort in the last verse. Jesus knows we all have different strengths and weaknesses, different experiences and hardships that lessen our power. So if one person seems to yield a hundred times in Christ's service, but another 'only' thirty, if that thirty is all she or he has, it is enough. Remember the widow's mite? Jesus does not force harsh comparisons between his disciples.

Contemplate which seed represents you at present; more importantly, what you can do to change from being the seed on the path or the one caught in the hedge. Pledge yourself today to one change in your prayer or social life which will give the seed a greater chance of flourishing.

As you desire to imitate him

Lord of parables, your seed is the message of the kingdom.
May I receive it with joy,
May it take root deep in my heart
And withstand all trouble or persecution,
Or shallow worldly temptation.
Then my service of you will flourish,
And yield to your glory.
Amen.

Proper 11

————◆◆◆————

Matthew 13.24–30, 36–43

Gaze – listen! to a radio station in France, or Spain, or Germany, or wherever you are on holiday or business. Perhaps you learnt that language at school and used to be proficient enough, but now you are rusty and only catch a little of what the speaker is saying. Imagine you're lost abroad and ask someone the way, but soon you're saying 'Slower, please, I don't understand'. Or you turn on a radio where there is a lot of interference and the voices drift away and nothing makes sense. Remember the confusion of talking on a mobile phone when the signal's fading or the other person is in a crowded room. You only catch a few words and try to piece together the meaning with only half the story. Feel the frustration of all these fragile means of communication.

Consider that in one way, Jesus' parables are like a fading radio signal, where we have to listen very keenly to grasp the truth. Yet consider how Jesus disguises unpalatable truths in simple, fireside stories. If we are lazy we can leave them at a childish level; but if we take them seriously, they force us to change our lives.

Consider how this parable builds on last week's. Both are obvious descriptions of normal farming practices and dilemmas. But this one introduces two more challenging points. Whereas last week's really made us look inward and judge ourselves, this one makes us look outwards. First, consider the devil, a most overlooked character in today's world. Beginning right back at the Fall, humanity has been struggling under the assault of temptations put in our path. Evil can at first sight be indistinguishable from good, as the weeds and wheat were similar as small shoots. It is only as they grow and show their fruits that we learn to distinguish between them.

The second theme counterpoints the first – it is not for us to make hasty judgements of who is good or evil. This surely warns us about trying to huddle into 'holier than thou' sects, and labelling others as unacceptable. We will only know at the proper time – the last judgement – who have been 'the sons [and daughters] of the kingdom'. The harvest, and the decisions, will be made by the reaper. But we can be sure that a judgement there will be.

Contemplate how you react when your best plans are spoiled by another's carelessness, folly or spite. Can you be patient enough to leave the outcome to God? What is more, contemplate the divisions within our churches and between churches, the sects that proliferate and the sad tendency we have to accuse the other of not honouring the truth. In the light of this parable, would it not be wise to let 'both grow together till the harvest?'

As you desire to imitate him

Lord, I long to shine in your kingdom
And not to be fooled by the tempter.
As all people grow together in one field
May I live as if I am the wheat
And not try to smother the weeds,
For who am I to judge another?
Amen.

Proper 12

———— •◦• ————

Matthew 13.31–33, 44–52

Gaze into the loft of an old house, left undisturbed by three or four generations of the same family. Feel the cobwebs brush against your face as you enter. Smell the dust and see it cake your hands. Begin to tidy up and sift through its contents. Slowly its secrets are revealed. There's an old Edwardian cot that would never pass today's Kitemark standards, and next to it a heap of battered suitcases full of faded ball gowns. Over there is a pile of lampshades that should have been thrown out years ago. Next, you find a wooden rocking horse that the grandchildren will love to play with once it's spruced up. Then you come across the real treasure – boxes of your grandparents' love letters and faded photos of your parents as children. Tucked away behind a cracked mirror you find even more family correspondence. Old mysteries about the family become clear: so that's what happened to Uncle Fred; or, no wonder Grandma was bitter! Though some of these old things have no future, others will breathe new life into you and bring you a fuller understanding of yourself. You have brought out of your storeroom new treasures, as well as old.

Consider how, now that Matthew's got started on the parables, he just can't stop! This breathless list of similes – 'the kingdom of God is like . . .' – at first glance is a jumble of ideas. But slow down and consider the key meaning of each. Summarize each in a word or two, and examine how they build on each other.

- In the mustard seed, Jesus tells us something small can become great.
- In the yeast, we see not only growth but transformation.
- In the treasure, we learn the kingdom is hidden, but infinitely desirable.

- In the pearl, the merchant searches, and gives up everything.
- In the fisher's net, the catch is full.

Though each simile is simple in itself, if we study the way they link together, we reach a vivid explanation of the kingdom, its joys and challenges. Though hidden, this kingdom is of great value (v. 46) and worth searching for and sacrificing for. The value of the kingdom lies in God's power to transform. This transformation may not always be pleasant, it can be disturbing, just as the fermentation of yeast is in the dough. The last parable, of the net full of fish, starts in the same hope of plenty, but has a sting in its tail – or perhaps its fin? For Jesus moves from all these positive uplifting images, to a less comfortable one. In fact, by verse 49 we are back with last week's message – there will be a time when the good and the bad will be judged, and the bad tossed back into the sea.

Contemplate finishing Jesus' sentence yourself: the kingdom of heaven is like . . .

How would you end it? What image from our world today would convey such transformation and value that you would sell all to gain it?

As you desire to imitate him

God of stories, breathe into me the truth
Behind your parables.
Direct me to search for the treasure
Hidden in your teaching,
That through the blessing of your wisdom
They may live afresh in my heart.
Amen.

Proper 13

Matthew 14.3–21

Gaze on this footsore crowd of people, who came out so enthusi-astically, traipsing in the midday sun from their town and villages over the hills, down steep stony paths, to the shore. See the men scanning the lake, shielding their eyes from the sun with their hand, eager to catch a glimpse of Jesus. 'There!' someone shouts, arm outstretched, pointing to a small sail no bigger than a gull. Hear the murmurs rise, 'He's coming, Jesus is coming', as they push forward with their sick to be nearer him as he steps ashore. The healing goes on for hours till the light begins to fade. The women begin to worry first, for it's way past supper time for the children. Now a different murmur rises from the crowd, more anxious than excited, more grumbling than supportive. How quickly the mood of a crowd can change! The disciples begin to worry: will this turn into a demon-stration, will the authorities get involved? 'Someone should do something,' they declare.

Consider the loneliness of Jesus. He has just heard of the brutal execution of 'the Baptist'. His face is worn and tired, and full of grief. Straight after John's disciples buried him, they went to Jesus. That might have been because as his cousin, he had the right to join in the mourning rituals. It might have been to warn him how much danger he now was in. It might have been for them to pledge themselves to him, for surely their main message was – you alone are our hope now; all the responsibility for reform and repentance rests on your shoulders. No longer did Jesus have a partner to share in this mission; he must carry the weight alone.

So Jesus had been drifting on the lake, trying to regain composure and hear the clear voice of God telling him what to do next. He must have craved peace and quiet. Instead, just as he arrived on the shore, he was met by this huge crowd. This was God's answer to his dilemma: 'Get on with what I expect you to do, Jesus; these people need you; heal them and feed them.' Jesus' compassion overruled his sorrow.

Consider how God's message is spelt out later, in verse 16, when Jesus teaches the disciples what God has just taught him: '*You* give them something to eat,' he says. It's no good thinking 'someone should do something'. It's up to us.

Contemplate how God so often works in this way. We fret and pray over what to do next and long for an unmistakable word, but instead God puts us into a situation which is itself the answer. Get on with it, he says.

Contemplate the dilemmas that weigh heavy on your mind or heart today, and look for the way God is expecting you to take responsibility.

As you desire to imitate him

Generous God, take my offerings and my actions,
However meagre and faltering.
Bless them in your service,
Break me in sacrifice if needs be,
Then share me with the world
Till your fullness abounds,
Through the example of your son, Jesus Christ.
Amen.

Proper 14

━━━━━◆◆◆◆━━━━━

Matthew 14.22–33

Gaze on a child taken swimming for the first time by her family. She's excited because she knows this is a treat, she's got a new swimsuit, and bright orange armbands. But once in the water, her excitement turns to fear. The first splash of her face makes her jump. She wraps her arms tightly around her father's neck, clinging on for safety. It is against all her experience to expect the water to hold her, for it parts at the smallest movement – how can something be solid and liquid at the same time? But gently the father prises her from him, and stretching his arms under her precious body, urges the child to 'Trust me. You can float. I'll never let you sink.'

Consider this passage, not as a promise that no one will ever drown again, or that coastguards and lifeboat heroes are redundant, but rather, as a graphic description of the curse of fear and the power of faith.

Consider the character of Peter, and how he stands for each one of us. We are told the Gospels are not biographies, but documents written with the specific purpose of arguing the case for Jesus' unique place in the history of the world. And yet, how strongly the character of Peter comes through, as in the best modern novel, revealing the inner man in all his confusion and complexity. Every time he appears he 'messes up', and here is no exception: a bold daredevil, impetuous but flawed, brave but foolish too. His devotion to Jesus is intense and as soon as he sees Jesus, he decides to brave the waves. It is almost as if he wants to test his faith, or perhaps he's showing off. The boat has been driven further out from shore than they'd expected. How many times have you had to face an experience knowing that the wind is against you? Walking one way along the seafront can be a pleasure, but then you turn and face into the wind and return home with head bowed and shoulders hunched, fighting for every step. Peter almost passes his challenge, till his 'little faith' gets the better of him. Though Peter lost faith in himself, Jesus never lost faith in Peter. While Peter confirms his humanity in this story, Jesus confirms his divinity: 'It is I,' he claims.

Consider next what had to happen for Peter to be rescued from drowning: he had to rely totally on Jesus and cry 'Lord, save me!' This is the spontaneous prayer that opens his heart wide enough for the power of Jesus to enter in.

Contemplate your fear of death and disaster. If you have already been near such an experience, recall it now. Remember your sense of helplessness. Then repeat quietly and urgently – 'Lord, save me.' And hear his reply – 'It is I.'

As you desire to imitate him

Protector God, I thank you
That before I even know I am in need
You come out and find me,
And when I am in danger
You are always within earshot.
When my faith is little, stretch out your hand.
Though I drown in sin, save me,
Through the power of him who rules the waves and the sea.
Amen.

Proper 15

———•◆•———

Matthew 15.[14–20] 21–28

Gaze on this woman. She is in great distress, and this gives her the courage to defy convention. Expecting to be rebuffed, she's got nothing to lose, so she may as well try. And at first, her fears are confirmed, as the disciples revile her and Jesus ignores her. Gaze on Jesus, turning his back on this woman, his lips sealed, his face stony. This is an unexpected picture of our Lord, grim, even grumpy. He's not only being unhelpful, he's unnecessarily rude, in effect describing this woman and her compatriots as dogs! Is he testing her, or has he really not yet understood himself the universality of his message? Watch the crowd nodding in agreement, the bolder ones shouting – how dare she! Look at the disciples close at hand, astonished at the woman's nerve.

Consider the significance of this story, placed here after last week's story of Peter. Then, Jesus' closest ally, who was destined to lead the Church, was admonished by Christ as 'you of little faith'. In contrast, in this week's story, we meet a stranger and a woman – second-class already because of her gender, and third-class because she is a pagan. And yet she wins this accolade from Christ: 'Woman, you have great faith.' So we learn again to find examples of faith in unexpected places and people.

Though a pagan, this woman respects Jesus as Lord and Son of David. Matthew's readers would have seen in this confirmation that, though gentiles can come to know Christ, they do so through the Jewish faith. In our modern time we do well to remember that our faith is rooted in Judaism.

Consider also that this passage follows a lengthy discourse by Jesus regarding what is clean and unclean (Matthew 15.1–20), ideas that were deeply rooted and significant in defining the Jewish identity. Jesus has argued a bolder definition, and rejected the narrow definitions and regulations that labelled people. And now, it seems, Jesus is faced with the logic of his own argument, and forced by this woman to take the step of including gentiles in his ministry. People of faith overturn the barriers between tribes and nations. Only our faith can make us clean.

Contemplate the pattern of prayer that this unnamed woman gifts to us. Her first words are 'Lord, have mercy', acknowledging her sinfulness and his authority, which she underlines by kneeling in submission. Her cry is then, 'Lord, help me!' Then, after she has listened to Jesus, she converses with him. She is determined to understand him, and tests his words with her reason. But it all begins with her faith.

As you desire to imitate him

Lord God of all peoples,
May I be open to your truth
In the voice of strangers,
And search for your wisdom
Among the excluded and oppressed,
And be willing to change my mind
As your Son did when the woman of Canaan
Sought you in faith.
Amen.

Proper 16

Matthew 16.13–20

Gaze on a stained-glass window, the sort you find in a large church or maybe a cathedral. It is covered with an array of prophets, often dressed in heavy bourgeois robes and fur hats, looking like successful merchants or stern academics. Their names are inscribed below them so that we should be able to pick them out and identify Elijah, Jeremiah, Moses, Ezekiel, Jonah and the rest. But to our eyes today, they appear very similar, and their stories and their prophecies are half forgotten. All the same, two pictures do stand out, for two peasant figures are always central to the window. One is a wild man dressed only in an animal skin, and we quickly guess he's John the Baptist. The other is Jesus, either in a plain, dull robe, or stripped naked, carrying the cross, unmistakable in his suffering. How is it that these two are allowed in with such eminences?

Consider the introduction here of the word 'church'. To come across it in the Gospels is a surprise; indeed this, and chapter 18, which we will come to in a few weeks, are the only times the word is used in Matthew, and it is debatable whether Jesus would actually have used it. We must also make our own mind up as to whether Jesus would have laid down such rules at such a stage of his ministry, or whether this is Matthew looking back from an evolving church.

Consider Peter again, named as founder of the Church because of his leap of faith, and given the keys of heaven. Consider the difference between these two charges, for it is dangerous to equate the Church with the kingdom of heaven. How well most of us know that our local church is flawed and fallible, just as Peter was. The church as an institution is of this world; the kingdom of heaven is that renewed world of God's power breaking through, which Jesus anticipated and taught us to pray for. When we misinterpret Jesus' pronouncement here and think that the Church is heavenly, we are prone to devote too much loyalty to a human institution. Much of the history of our religion is marred by the conflict that stems from this confusion. The church is necessary, but reliance on a mere institution cannot open the gates of heaven.

Consider then why Peter was given the keys of heaven. The words that follow are much debated: were the keys to unlock the kingdom to gentiles on the day of Pentecost? In what way do they bind or loose? Does this give Peter authority to pronounce guilt and innocence? These almost legal terms have introduced great distress into our institutions, allowing excommunications and charges of heresy. Consider whether Jesus really would have given Peter that sort of power, when his whole teaching has been implying that it is faith that opens doors and God's mercy that forgives.

Contemplate the local church in which you worship. Contemplate with thankfulness the signs within it which show it is building up the kingdom of heaven. Contemplate the font where children are welcomed, and the lectern where the Bible rests, and the pulpit where God's truths are explored, and the choir where people sing God's praises and the pews where his people join in the worship of God; contemplate the table where they share the bread and wine. Contemplate the main entrance to your church. Does it open inwards, or outwards?

As you desire to imitate him

Son of the living God, you ask me to decide who you are:
I say you are Son of Man, my pattern for living;
I say you are prophet, inspiration for the way ahead;
I say you are the brother always by my side;
I say you are the anointed one, the Christ,
I say you are the saviour of all.
Amen.

Proper 17

—•◦•—

Matthew 16.21–28

Gaze on Peter dragging Jesus off to a corner of the room where they are lodging, and Jesus and Peter standing with their backs to the rest of the group, as Peter berates him! Or perhaps this episode took place as they were walking along on their return from Caesarea Philippi, and a confused Peter drops his impatient step to keep pace with Jesus, pulls him by his sleeve and whispers urgently. Like in a silent film, see their expressions – Peter's earnest bluster and bad-tempered rebuke – you shall never be defeated! See Jesus' face change from an open concerned listening, to anger. Then Peter steps back as if slapped in the face: for his Master to reject him like this and label him his adversary is more than his passionate nature can bear.

Consider how many of Jesus' parables are about loss and search. The story of the lost sheep and the lost coin are all about someone searching for love's sake – the shepherd and the old woman stand in for God. These stories we are happy to read to our children, for they both have happy endings – the sheep is recovered, the coin found, all is restored and the world goes on as it did before. But now Jesus is not talking in parables, and instead of a sheep or a coin, it is a life that is to be lost; first of all Jesus' own (v. 21) and then his disciples' (v. 25). This is less comfortable and no wonder Peter exploded with outrage. He is focused on the fear of loss, and forgets what it is that Jesus wanted them to search for.

Here Jesus is announcing the destiny which has slowly become clear to him; but the disciples can't take it in and don't seem to remember these predictions till sometime after the crucifixion and resurrection. Though Jesus spoke in simple terms, their hearts would not accept what their ears heard. We cannot blame the disciples for misunderstanding, for they just could not tally such disgrace and tragedy with their understanding of God's ultimate victory and glory. Nothing in their lives or religion had prepared them for this reversal, and in truth we are still trying to unravel this mystery today.

Jesus accused Peter of being a stumbling block – and when we trip over a stumbling block, we lose our footing. Jesus had kept upright when tempted by Satan in the wilderness. Perhaps that was what he was remembering when he called out 'Get behind me, Satan!' Surely, he must have thought, he'd passed beyond temptation. Yet temptation can appear in many guises.

Contemplate your soul: what do you mean by the word? Are you a divided self, body and spirit? Surely, the purpose of Jesus' saving work was to integrate the body and soul into one complete self who truly reflects the nature of Jesus and image of God, who so truly imitates him in faith and actions that she or he will be willing to give their life away.

As you desire to imitate him

Dear Lord, put into my mind the things of God
And banish the misunderstandings of human beings;
May I never be a stumbling block to the faith of others,
But be willing to exchange the temporal for the eternal
And give up my profit for the kingdom's gain.
Amen.

Proper 18

————— ·•·•·•· —————

Matthew 18.15–20

Gaze on a heated discussion in Parliament, with opposing sides interrupting and jeering at each other and the Speaker calling out in vain 'Order! Order!' Watch a row between two children, brothers and sisters, running to Mum or Dad: 'He [or she] started it!' Listen to a more restrained argument at work, where discussions get heated as people cling to entrenched positions and refuse to budge. It doesn't take much to extend the picture to international conflict, where war and violence erupt and all possibility of peaceful persuasion is lost. The arguments, some of which have tragic consequences, all have one thing in common – people have stopped listening to each other.

Consider this passage as a bridge looking looking back into Deuteronomy and Leviticus with their rules about handling disputes and the need for witnesses, and looking forward to the early Church and its way of organizing disagreements. Here we have Matthew's second and final mention of 'Church' (see Proper 16) and the whole sound of this passage has much more of a feeling of Acts about it. The old Jewish rules are modified here by the Christian imperative to treat the sinner with patience and to carry on talking. And if one may dare criticize the Lord, it may be added that listening should be a two-way activity: those in authority should also listen to the point of view of the sinner. In mediation both sides may feel offended, and agreement will only slowly emerge when each side truly understands the other. There is an old saying – 'to know all, is to forgive all'. And to be in the position of knowing the background, the reasons, the history and the motives of someone, there must first have been an awful lot of patient listening. Jesus himself knew this, which is why this piece has a less authentic ring to it, for had he not listened to the Canaanite woman (Proper 15) and in the end changed his mind? Jesus in fact gathered in the pagan and the tax collector, he did not excommunicate them.

Consider how the heretics of one century often become accepted in the next; Luther and Wesley immediately spring to mind. The Church would do well to consider very carefully indeed before it excludes or excommunicates anyone.

Contemplate what is missing from this description: it is any mention of love. For that we turn to today's epistle (Romans 13.8–14) and the passage, 'Let no debt remain outstanding, except the continuing debt to love one another, for he who loves his fellow-man has fulfilled the law.' When the rigid legal structures of challenging wrongdoing are injected with love, true reconciliation can flourish.

Contemplate one situation known to you that is in need of mediation. Hold both sides in your prayers.

As you desire to imitate him

Lord Jesus, our mediator,
Judge us with love and rebuke us with mercy,
And mediate between those of us who disagree.
Today I pray for all homes, workplaces and nations
Where accusations lead to conflict,
That each side will listen to the other
And learn to love again.
Amen.

Proper 19

———•◦•———

Matthew 18.21–35

Gaze on the king in this story. It appears from the context that he's an eastern potentate ruling over a world where slavery is common and torture rife. Perhaps he's just entered a prolonged war, or the harvest has been poor, or he wants to build a new palace. Whatever the reason, he is in grave need of cash and so decides to call in his debts. Gaze on the fear in the eyes of the man brought to him, who owed such an immense fortune, maybe borrowed when times were good. But now he's fallen on ill health, or his ship has sunk in a violent storm. He knows that at best he will be sold into slavery and at worst executed for his failure, which could be seen as treason. He makes no excuses but throws himself on the mercy and patience of the king. And the king does not interrogate him or lay down restrictions as to what he can spend his money on and how he must arrange his finances in future before he'll consider remitting the debt. This is a king with a merciful heart.

Consider how this parable alters the harshness of last week's reading, which it directly follows. Here, Jesus tells us to forgive 'seventy times seven', in other words, without limit. In this outline of forgiveness, the parable shows that the only precondition for forgiveness is that we should be prepared to forgive too. Here we have the core of the Lord's Prayer told to us in story form: 'and forgive us our sins as we forgive those who sin against us'. So this reading should modify our response to last week's more formal process. Consider too, that Jesus gives this story the full authority of his Father: 'The kingdom of heaven is like [this] king.'

This parable takes on new meaning in today's world, where 'Make Poverty History' and other campaigns have urged rich Western governments to release the poor nations, mainly in Africa, from their debts. These debts were built on dubious arrangements that benefited the donor as much as the recipient, often tying them into commitments to use certain contractors or develop certain raw materials or export goods that their own population was badly in need of. There has been some progress towards the cancelling of such debts, but how slow and how niggardly and how cautious it has been!

Contemplate the connection between the words *sin* and *debt*. This story of debt is used to answer Peter's question about forgiveness of sin. Some translations of the Lord's Prayer use sin and others prefer debt. For when we feel that others have sinned against us, it is usually a hurt they have caused, and the least we feel is that they 'owe' us an apology, some compensation for the harm. That is what we are called upon to let go of. Contemplate a world where the demand for justice is secondary to forgiveness, which would be a world where righteousness prevails.

As you desire to imitate him

Merciful King, I pray for all in debt,
For people who cannot pay their mortgages,
And for countries who owe vast sums,
And cannot build schools or hospitals.
Soften my heart with your compassion
That I may work to release such people
From the burden of debt and fear of destitution.
Amen.

Proper 20

Matthew 20.1–16

Gaze on that very British pastime, a queue. We queue for buses, we queue at the checkout, and we wait patiently in line to buy our ticket at the cinema. Remember the old-fashioned system in banks and post offices? The first to arrive could easily end up the last to be served, as you had to guess which was the fastest-moving queue and attach yourself to it, only to see your neighbour gliding past while you were still stuck behind someone renewing their passport and car tax together. Then impatiently you dash to another queue only to fume when that one grinds to a halt as the assistant goes off on a coffee break. Listen to the grumbles change to anger when someone queue-jumps!

Then look at these desperate labourers in the Mediterranean heat, crouching on the ground in the shade of a great cork tree, getting thirstier, getting dustier, but resigned to waiting for ages more. Skip to the end of this story – they are chosen to be paid first! They expect a penny, but into their dirty, sweaty palm, the steward puts a pound.

Consider the landowner's question, which is God's question: 'Are you envious because I am generous?' (v. 15). This good employer makes sure all his employees earn enough to support their families. How can that be wrong? And what does that tell us about our modern economy when some people earn billions, while others struggle on 'the minimum wage'? As in last week's story, we are challenged to see a compassionate economy based on righteousness. Yet when we read this story, the British fairness gene resists and argues – it's just not fair!

Consider what this story is a response to – nothing less than Peter's question 'Who then can be saved?' (Matthew 19.25), and the disciples' understandable complaint 'We have left everything to follow you! What then will there be for us?' (v. 27). But Jesus tells them, and us, 'The kingdom of heaven is like this.' What unwelcome news to us fair-minded Brits! We expect to gain from our efforts in proportion to that which we put in, and we expect God to abide by our rules too. Consider God's indiscriminate generosity and ask yourself if you can act that way too, and not keep a tally of everything owed to you. We must fix our eyes straight ahead on our own relationship with God, and not look sideways at the luck of others.

Contemplate what we mean when we describe someone as being 'gracious' – they are attractive, considerate, courteous, and they enhance and enrich those whom they meet. The unmerited favour of God shown in this parable is another word for this graciousness. Let us contemplate the grace of God and let us be grateful (note that the two words share the same root!). Let us imitate God's graciousness in our lives. Contemplate what it means 'to give way with good grace'.

As you desire to imitate him

Gracious God, help me accept
I will not always be rewarded
For hard work or loving actions.
It is not for me to demand love from you
Or desire to do better than my neighbour.
I long for the time when we stand before you in the kingdom
And all join hands in a circle of love.
Amen.

Proper 21

Matthew 21.23–32

Gaze on this family scene, played out daily in thousands of households throughout the world. Supper's over and the mother says to the oldest child, 'Can you help me with the dishes?' The child continues to scrape his plate for the last of the custard and pretends he hasn't heard. But Mum's wise to that ruse, and says again, 'Can you help me with the dishes tonight?' Not many children will be as brave as the son in Jesus' story and come out with a forthright NO. Rather he'll toss about in his mind which excuse to try tonight – it better be something new. 'Oh, Mum, but I've got so much homework to do.' Won't that surely fool her? A more honest reply might be, 'But Ben's coming round later and we were going to watch a DVD', when he really means he doesn't want to be caught in the kitchen. But the truthful answer would be, 'I just don't want to put your needs before my own pleasure.'

Listen to the second son in Jesus' story, and decide if there is much difference. 'I will, sir,' he says, thinking, 'I'll do it later, when I've finished what I want to do.' So of course he never gets round to it, because his own priorities always take precedence.

Consider how in this story it is the wayward child who finally helps. Jesus means us to see in this the marginalized and the sinners who responded to his message more easily than the comfortable conformers. Was that because they had less to lose? Consider how both sons' behaviours stem from the same old fault of human nature. Most of the time, most of us put our own desires and comfort before that of others, because we simply see ourselves as the centre of the world and can't or won't put ourselves in another's shoes. Consider what fundamentally lies behind the Ten Commandments and Jesus' 'new commandment' – it is a reversal of that human self-centredness, and an appeal to put the other first.

Consider what is the source of the moral authority that governs your decisions. Where does ultimate authority come from – is it from heaven, or from human beings (vv. 25, 26)? Do you agree with the opinion that without religion – a belief in God – nothing is absolute and everything relative, and therefore any authority rests within one's own self? Atheists quite understandably baulk at the crude suggestion that they do not have a set of honourable, reliable guidelines for their life. However, it is also possible that they underestimate the fact that until recently, our world has been completely imbued with belief in God, so that we cannot say what commandments – if any – we might have agreed upon without him.

Contemplate your values – are they rock-solid signposts that always govern your actions, or do you let superficial preferences affect your choices? Contemplate your conscience – that in-built alarm bell that rings when you know you are acting against your most deeply held values, and disobeying the authority of God. Have you heard it ring recently?

As you desire to imitate him

Righteous God, each Sunday in church
I acknowledge your authority,
But I often ignore your promptings during the week.
When I waver, prick my conscience,
When I follow false paths, turn me around,
When I choose to give my desire precedence,
Remind me of the true values
Taught to me by your Son.
Amen.

Proper 22

―•―

Matthew 21.33–46

Gaze, not on this story, but another scene of attack, that will take place a little later in Matthew's Gospel, when the violence predicted here against the son and heir finally takes place. Gaze as the 'tenants' approach him in Gethsemane with swords and clubs, as if he's a rebel, to be arrested. Hear Jesus exclaim, not without irony, 'Am I leading a rebellion?' Gaze at him bound by the temple guard, the rope cutting deep into his wrists. Stare at his back, bloody and raw from the flogging. See him stripped of his clothes, humiliated in his nakedness. Look at the scratches and wounds. See his scalp where the crown of thorns was rammed on his head. Do not look away. Does he flinch when he's spat at and struck? One degradation follows another. All this before the actual murder – the death sentence – is carried out.

Consider the difference in meaning between the words 'rebellion' and 'revolution'. The first means open resistance to an established authority that is more or less legitimate and more or less benign, and such rebels often appropriate for themselves not just the power but the privilege and lifestyle of those they have overthrown. But revolution means the overthrow of a social order in favour of a totally new system, with a fundamental break with the past and ordered on a different set of principles. Examine this story and it is easy to work out the identity of the rebels, for the tenants rebel against the owner and, it would appear, for no good reason. There is no clue that the owner is repressive or tyrannical, just that he is expecting to collect his portion of the produce as rent. Rather, we see that it is the rebels' avarice that makes them want to grab the inheritance from the son. It is their wilfulness and refusal to honour the terms of their agreement with the owner, not any provocation by him, that causes the rebellion.

The rebels – we ourselves – tear up their tenancy agreement and attempt to usurp the owner, and go it alone.

Consider who is the revolutionary here. We will look in vain for a Che Guevara character in the plot. No, the overthrow of the social order is brought about by God, and the new system which is brought in is brought in by God. God brings upheaval to our social norms and reversal of our expectations. This is the third story in a row that starts when those who might have expected due reward lose their chance by their own behaviour; and ends with the surprise of a new people being blessed by God's bounty.

Contemplate our rebelliousness; starting with Adam and Eve, the Old Testament is a catalogue of God's people's rejection of God's will. Contemplate the threat in v. 43 – 'the kingdom of God will be taken away from you and given to a people who will produce its fruit'. That threat still stands today, if we rebel. That threat still stands today, if we fail to produce fruit.

As you desire to imitate him

Master of the vineyard,
May I abide by the terms of your covenant
And never seek to usurp your authority
Or rebel against your will.
May I be worthy of the trust you've put in me,
Always ready to respect your Son
And to return to you the praise and honour due.
Amen.

Proper 23

Matthew 22.1–14

The day nobody came to my party.

Gaze on the one character in this story who has nothing to say: the bridegroom. He's dressed in all his finery, proud and anxious, for tomorrow is his big day when he'll meet his bride, possibly for the first time. The banquet is in his honour, but where are the guests? Where are his friends, his cousins, and the children he grew up with? The waiters stand around staring straight ahead, their trays full of untouched glasses of champagne slowly losing their fizz; the band tries to liven the evening up with a tune, but sounds flat. The prince looks at the clock – the invitation was for 8 and he knows no one wants to be the first to arrive, but it's 9.30 now and still no one's turned up. Has he lived all his life under the false assumption that people cared for him? But surely, if not for his sake, they would come out of respect for his father.

Consider where the real clue to this passage lays – just a few verses earlier, at the end of chapter 21 (v. 45), 'when the Chief Priests and Pharisees heard Jesus' parables, they knew he was talking about them'. Now we see clearly that the invited stand for the leaders of the age who should have been the first to recognize the authority of Jesus. Yet not only do they rebuff the king, but they turn on his servants and ill-treat them – they are positively working against the kingdom. This story and last week's are, in fact, a pair.

In case we too easily conclude we're not like the Pharisees, and identify ourselves with everyone else, and think that is our ticket to the kingdom, Jesus warns that even those not expecting the invitation must be in a state of readiness.

Consider the other layer of meaning in this story, for it is the wedding feast of the son, and so Jesus is signalling his own status to the chief priests, which must have maddened them even further.

These parables told by Jesus in this last period in Jerusalem, when the threat to him was growing, are fraught with warnings that are meant to burst our complacency, and we are called to find ourselves in these stories, and respond to the promise of the kingdom of heaven, which is another way of saying the kingdom of God.

Contemplate how many feasts and banquets Jesus has told us about in these readings, yet how rarely we are excited by the good news that the kingdom will be like a party. Remember the excitement you felt as a child when you were getting ready to go to a birthday party? That is the excitement we should feel at the prospect of the kingdom. Our restlessness and suspicion and worldliness make us look elsewhere for delights, when all the time God is longing to prepare a table for us. Picture that table, full of all your favourite foods, and Jesus taking you by the hand and leading you to the place of honour at the top table.

As you desire to imitate him

Father, you invited me to your feast
And offered me a place in your kingdom,
But I was too busy to come.
You even came out to look for me
As I was hurrying down the street.
Help my heart be dressed with longing
And my will be clothed in readiness
To say yes to the delights of the banquet of your Son.
Amen.

Proper 24

————— •◆• —————

Matthew 22.15–22

Gaze on the threatening circle tightening around Jesus that we see in these passages. Jesus has walked into the lion's den and is challenging the Pharisees and the Temple authorities face to face. Here we are entering the longest week of his life, between Palm Sunday and Easter Day, when he meets with the powerful and privileged and keeps sparking controversy. Like a boxer going every round in the boxing ring, Jesus keeps coming back for more trouble, and every time his opponents think they'd dealt the final knockout blow, Jesus springs up from his corner with renewed vigour and shrewd tactics. No wonder his opponents lost patience in the end.

Consider the arguments that take place at every election in Great Britain – should our taxes be higher or lower? It is a brave (or foolish) politician who openly argues to raise taxes. All parties vie with each other to pretend they'll bring the greatest common benefit out of the lowest individual contribution. We are all so good at identifying what we want the money spent on. 'Why don't they?' trips off our tongue, but we yell if our own tax bill rises. No one seems able to proclaim taxation as 'a good thing'.

In a complex society where you can never know all your neighbours, and never know whose need is greatest, taxation is the best way of channelling what you can afford – the coat you can give away – to house a homeless family, build safer roads, or provide a hospital bed for an elderly person.

The Pharisees spoke more wisely than they realized when they described Jesus in verse 16 as 'a man of integrity . . . you aren't swayed by men because you pay no attention to who they are'. Jesus' concern was only ever for people's needs, and not their status. We so need politicians today whom we can trust like that. But we also have the great privilege of living in a democracy. Consider how the downtrodden Israelites would have welcomed the vote! So it is up to our integrity to choose wise leaders, and if they fail, we have the liberty to dismiss them – just think how much the Jews would have loved the right and freedom to get rid of the Romans!

Contemplate what in your life is 'of God': your life itself, your health, your talents and intelligence, maybe the gift of good relationships. All these must be rendered to God as our taxation, so that he can use them, through us, for the good of our sisters and brothers.

As you desire to imitate him

Lord of this world, guard my integrity when I come to vote.
Help me consider the needs of everyone,
And not just my family,
When I make my decision.
May I not be swayed by false promises,
Nor our leaders be swayed by popularity or power
But rule in accordance with your truth.
Amen.

Proper 25

───◦•◦───

Matthew 22.34–46

Gaze on a religious community, set deep in the isolated countryside, where monks or nuns live together all their lives, and must learn to 'get on'. Look around at the places set on the long refectory table, and place yourself there. Study the faces of the visitors: wayfarers, stopping in for a meal; people recovering from addictions, or a broken heart, or cancer. Young people are there, on the verge of breakdown, and elderly who are bereft and bereaved. Some are smartly dressed, but others wear stained jumpers or torn trousers. The person next to you smells and the one on the other side can't stop tapping her fingers on the table – her anxiety is palpable. The stranger opposite you starts up in banal chatter, when all you want is peace and quiet. Such communities test the meaning of the second commandment to destruction. Place God at this table.

Consider how Jesus has turned the tables on his detractors. They've goaded and tested him enough, first about Caesar and their taxes, then about marriage at the resurrection, and finally they aimed straight at the central laws of their faith. Jesus has batted the ball back, striking fours and sixes to their amazement every time. For when he's asked what is the greatest commandment in the law, the very first word of his reply is *love*. This love is a verb and not just a noun. He rejects neither human law nor God's law, but transforms and completes them. He says nothing exactly new but the combination is dramatic.

Consider Jesus' great ability to disagree politely, and argue in a kindly manner, and talk softly to his opponents. Consider how you cope in an argument. Do you cringe and clam up, or do you too easily become aggressive and dismissive of the other's point of view?

Consider how Jesus coped with criticism – always calmly, often by a question, as he took the idea further and deeper than anyone expected, often in an entirely different direction. And now it's his turn to bowl a ball straight at them and see if they've the brains or insight to answer – 'What do you think about the Christ – whose son is he?'

Contemplate the best way of winning an argument, not just to score a cheap point and come out feeling on top, but really to effect a lasting change on another person's attitude. Bring before God one person or group with whom you disagree. Let God search out your motives, for we must be certain before we try to change another's mind.

Contemplate where there are opportunities in your life to ask the question that will lodge deep in another's mind, and lead them to God.

As you desire to imitate him

I promise to love you, Lord God,
With all my heart – all my compassion,
With all my soul – all my prayer,
With all my mind – all my reason.
And with all these powers,
I will love my neighbour as myself.
Amen.

SUNDAYS BEFORE ADVENT

The Fourth Sunday before Advent

Matthew 24.1–14

Gaze on a bombsite, in Baghdad, perhaps, or maybe you're old enough to remember the rubble in our cities after the Second World War, a newsreel of Dresden, or the wreck of Hiroshima. Homes have collapsed, spires have tumbled and crypts are exposed, so that everything is flat and unrecognizable. Not one stone is left on another, everything is thrown down. Once-proud banks have been exposed and destroyed, glass has shattered and scattered everywhere. The street plan is lost, and you wander aimlessly with no sense of direction, or hope of finding a landmark. Rats scavenge in the heaps of stone and brick and broken timbers, but there is nothing that a human can gain from being here. When this city does come to be rebuilt, it will look quite different.

Consider verse 12 – 'because of the increase of wickedness, the love of most will grow cold'. Consider how evil is contagious, how extremists in early 1930s Germany had infected a huge population five years later, or how the hatred in South Africa under apartheid meant many otherwise decent people closed down their compassion for a whole group of people. Fear overruled love and they worshipped power.

But also consider the few, whose love does not grow cold. What is the difference between people who do not bend to the prevailing dogma, and will not sacrifice their compassion? They are Christ-like in their openness to others and their belief that we are all God's children. Though they are handed over to be persecuted and even executed, they stand firm for the gospel values, knowing that to compromise them is to compromise their soul. Where does such courage come from? It can only be 'superhuman', we say. These remarkable people keep the light of love burning in dire times and teach those who come after them to know the difference between false prophets and the word of God.

Now we have left behind the controversies that occurred at the end of Jesus' life, and turned to darker controversies still, relating to the end of time, as we approach the end of our church year.

Contemplate the collapse of time in this reading. Contemplate the vast distances of space that astronomers have made visible to us, and the sight of stars formed at the beginning of time. Contemplate the whole cosmos as it expands to the end of time. Our minds can't understand infinity; we hope for eternity but can't grasp its form, and yet Jesus seems so at ease with all these difficult ideas.

Contemplate how Christ is the birth-pang – the beginning, the Alpha, but also the sign of the end – the Omega.

As you desire to imitate him

Lord of the beginning and the end,
May my love for you never grow cold.
Help me to reject false prophets
And stand firm for the gospel,
And so be a witness to all the nations,
That you are Christ, Alpha and Omega.
Amen.

The Third Sunday before Advent

Matthew 25.1–13

Gaze on an early Saturday morning in late summer, when the sun has come up and promises a glorious day. You open the curtains and delight at the weather – it is perfect for planting your bulbs for next spring; perfect for feeding the earth and making it ready. But first there is the bath and hair wash to do, and then the leisurely cup of coffee and the newspaper to read. Then a few chores just to make the house tidy and a couple of phone calls to make. Next time you look out of the window, the sun is nowhere to be seen. In fact storm clouds are brewing and the first spots of rain spatter windowpanes. Another typical British day! Your opportunity is lost; now your plants and bulbs will never be planted; and if not planted, they'll never grow; and if they don't grow, they'll never bloom.

Consider how this story enlarges on the disciples' question last week: 'Tell us, when will this [end of the age] happen?' How much they'd have liked to know. In every aspect of our life, we want to know what's round the corner. How often we cry 'If I only had known'. Consider the common denominator in so many of Jesus' stories that we have heard during this church year. It is the challenge to be ready to act now, for we are on the brink of judgement. Think back again to the story of the guests at the wedding feast and how they lost their chance by dallying.

Consider what it means to be wise or foolish. A wise person listens and learns, and looks ahead. A foolish person doesn't learn from past experience and looks only for short-term gain. Their mantra is 'Oh dear, I just wasn't thinking.'

A wise person operates with lots of words that begin with P: they have priorities because they know they can't do everything; they are prepared; they keep their needs and desires in proportion, and have a proper perspective on their worries and woes. In face of problems, they are positive. But a foolish person is ill equipped and ill disciplined and therefore ill prepared and ill at ease, and will panic rather than plan. They are often over-optimistic, not caring to weigh things in the balance, but hoping for the best, just like these foolish women. Or, alternatively, they allow pessimism to freeze their will.

Contemplate how good you are at waiting. Are you a naturally patient person, or do you feel your stomach tighten with frustration whenever you have to queue? Contemplate how you can best live in a waiting attitude, expectant but calm, hopeful but realistic, prepared and patient, energetic but not distracted.

As you desire to imitate him

God of time, God in time,
As I wait to welcome the Son of God
Grant me light to keep watch by.
Since I do not know the hour of your coming,
May I not close the door
But keep open the window of my heart
So that the Holy Spirit may enter in.
Amen.

The Second Sunday before Advent

---◆·◆·◆---

Matthew 24.14–30

Gaze on a man with a metal detector, slowly inching across a field or a beach, searching for buried treasure. Sometimes he'll turn up an odd Roman coin, or a Tudor brooch, or a broken pot. But occasionally someone hits the jackpot and finds a hoard of Anglo-Saxon gold and silver, hidden, centuries ago, by someone in a time of conflict, worried that if they were invaded by the enemy, they would lose all their wealth. So in the dead of night they went out into the woods or down to the end of their garden, took a spade and dug deep into the clay. There they left their treasure. There they lost their treasure, all because they were afraid.

Consider it is no coincidence that the English word for a special attribute or gift is the same as the Aramaic unit of currency – a talent. It derives exactly from this parable, another example of the great influence of the Bible on our language and our thought. Consider this story as the third in the series we have heard, about the signs of the end of time, and how we are to behave until then, in active waiting. We should not just take from this story the warning about laziness or fear, but must learn to look to the horizon of the end of time, which is the real focus of these stories we study up to Advent.

Having thought about the ten virgins last week, we know now the difference between wisdom and folly, so we can examine these three servants and ask ourselves which acted wisely, and which foolishly? By now we know that the values of Jesus' kingdom are not always straightforward, and can be counter-intuitive. In the light of the 2008/09 global financial disaster, where greed and speculation ran riot, and investments were definitely not safe, we might well applaud the third servant for his care and caution! But we must remember that in all Jesus' teaching, there is the imperative that we *grow*. We must grow in confidence and leadership, in fluency about our faith, and openness to others, so that as we develop, so does the kingdom. We must not stay stuck in a rut of inertia, timidity and social conformity. And so the wisdom comes in knowing how best to use our talents, and when maybe we are expected to take a risk for God's sake.

Contemplate these words from Proverbs 6.10–11, as a warning against folly and complacency: 'a little sleep, a little slumber, a little folding of the hands to rest, and poverty will come on you like a bandit and scarcity like an armed man.' Contemplate what part of your life right now God wants you to invest your time and talents into.

As you desire to imitate him

Master, may I be faithful with the responsibility
You have entrusted to me
And active with the gifts you have given me.
As your hope is for me to grow
In love and wisdom and commitment,
Let me not hide or slumber,
But be faithful until your return.
Amen.

Christit the King

—◆◦◆—

Matthew 25.31–46

Gaze on all these people gathering before the Son of Man on the day of judgement, all the characters we've met over the year. There are kings from the east and an innkeeper; there's Mary, mother of Jesus, and Joseph her husband; chief priests and scribes and Pharisees, Pilate and Herod and Caiphas. Then there's Peter – so many times, usually getting things wrong, and the disciples, still arguing about who gets to sit at Jesus' right hand; Judas, Nicodemus and Matthew the tax collector, the many times married Samaritan woman at the well, and the woman of Canaan, who refused to be treated as a dog; lots and lots of children, the hungry five thousand and countless number of the harassed, the helpless and the sick. Each time they've encountered Jesus has been decision-time for them. They've been challenged by him to act, to put the other first, to show faith and turn away from fear. And those who followed him learnt the cost of love.

Consider that now we have reached the end of our church year we are back where we started, with the judgement of the approaching kingdom. We've just finished reading the whole of Matthew 25 in these weeks up to Advent, and this parable is the third story in the sequence. Let us remember how over the last few weeks we've thought about the signs of the end of the age and concentrated on people learning to show a readiness for the kingdom. Now this final story is about the moment of its arrival. And this is where the inescapability of judgement is overwhelming. Matthew builds up the drama and crisis of the threat of this judgement by Jesus' repeated use of the words 'I was, I was, I was . . .', and the question posed by the so called-righteous in reply, 'When, when, when?'

It is interesting to realize that the descriptions of how Jesus expects us to behave do not actually mention the word love, but give concrete examples of what love in action looks like. All Jesus' ministry has been a model of love in action – love the verb, and not some vague state of warm good feeling.

Consider the festival we celebrate the day – Christ the King, the unique King we have in Jesus. Here is a throne and a king but not like any one we've ever seen in history.

This king's strength lies in his deep care for each of his subjects, with whom he identifies as his equal in need. This is a king who gives away his power and shares his inheritance, and yet is still he 'who fills everything in every way' (Ephesians 1.23, from the epistle set for today). Being a king does not make you God; but being God includes being a king.

Contemplate the past year and ask yourself where you have been of use to others, and where you have helped others to survive or grow or heal. There has been no point in gazing on Jesus in the Gospels, or considering his words, or contemplating his glory, if we have not grown to be more like him in thought, and word and deed.

As you desire to imitate him

Son of Man, and King of all,
I bow my head to your judgement
And I lift up my heart to you
In thanksgiving for your gospel of good news.
In serving others, may I serve you
And in serving you, grow into your likeness,
And so be welcomed into your eternal kingdom.
Amen.